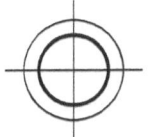

Table of Contents

TARGETED KILLING

Self-Defense, Preemption, and the War on Terrorism

THOMAS B. HUNTER

ISBN: 1-4392-5205-X
ISBN-13: 9781439252055
Library of Congress Control Number: 2009907737

Visit www.booksurge.com to order additional copies.

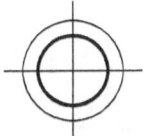

Acknowledgements

This book is dedicated to my parents, Larry and Sue Werner, whose support over the years has enabled me to experience many wonderful places and people and facilitated my academic, professional, and personal growth. Without them, and the support of my sister Ellen Mai and brother Eric Werner, this book would not have been possible. Finally, I would like to thank Mike and Laura Hunter for their support over the years.

I would also like to thank Mr. Gary Greco and Mr. Darrell Nolen for their professional guidance and support. Their mentorships at different stages in my career were the cornerstones of my development as an intelligence analyst. I would not be the writer I am today without their supervision and direction.

I would also be grossly remiss if I did not thank Dr. Thom Montgomery for his advice and insight, which has also been an essential part of my personal growth.

I would like to acknowledge the University of St. Andrews, Scotland, and the faculty of the International Security Studies (ISS) program, under whose guidance this book was researched and written. Particularly, I would like to thank Dr Magnus Ranstorp who served as my graduate advisor and remains today one of the preeminent experts on international terrorism.

Finally, I would also like to thank Henley-Putnam University for agreeing to the publication, in book format, of the paper that originally appeared in the university's *Journal of Strategic Security* (May 2009).

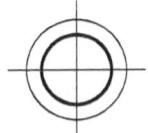

Summary

This book assesses the parameters and utility of 'targeted killing' in combating terrorism and its role within the norm of state self-defence in the international community. The author's thesis contends that, while targeted killing provides states with a potentially effective method of combating terrorism, is inherently limited, sometimes dangerous, and not a panacea for all the challenges confronting counterterrorism policy and practice. The adoption and execution of such a program brings with it, among other potential pitfalls, political repercussions, and other related, and often unanticipated complications.

Targeted killing is defined herein as the premeditated, preemptive, and intentional killing of an individual or individuals known or believed to represent a present and/or future threat to the safety and security of a state through affiliation with terrorist groups or individuals.

The principle conclusions of this book are that targeted killing:

- Must be wholly differentiated from 'assassination' and related operations involving the intentional targeting of an individual during wartime, in order to be considered properly and rationally;

- Is a politically risky undertaking with potentially negative international implications;
- The proven desire of some terrorist groups to conduct attacks involving mass casualties against innocent civilians may, in the future, cause states to reconsider previous abstention from adopting targeted killing in order to protect their populace;
- Can serve to impact terrorists and terrorist groups on a strategic, operational, and tactical level;
- This impact has historically proven both negative and (unintentionally) positive for terrorist groups; and,
- Oftentimes exposes civilians to unintentional harm.

The methods of investigation include a thorough review of the available literature (to include books, published and unpublished essays, interviews of selected individuals (to include academics and retired members of military and police forces), and the author's independent analysis.

*Killing a man is murder unless you
do it to the sound of trumpets. - Voltaire*

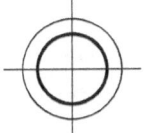

Introduction

This book examines the dynamic of 'targeted killing' as it relates to the phenomenon of modern international terrorism and the individual state's rights to self-defence.

Due to the nature of modern international terrorism, particularly in its suicide form, and its emergence on the world stage primarily after the September 11 2001 attacks, academic focus on this type of potential response—targeted killing—has been limited. Consequently, this book endeavors to contribute an essentially new and largely unexplored insight into targeted killing as it pertains to the state's right to defend its citizens.

Given the paucity of scholarly study on targeted killing, and the natural reluctance of nations to acknowledge any formal policy, there is relatively little published literature (aside from a small number of essays appearing primarily in academic journals) against which to balance the findings and conclusions presented in this book. The bulk of the available literature used as reference material herein was derived from works pertaining to related topics, such as assassination, conventional and unconventional warfare, counterterrorism, and the norm of state self-defence. This book also makes extensive use of case studies involving groups (for example, HAMAS, Irish Republican Army [IRA] etc.) and cites both 'covert' and 'overt' state policy as employed over the last 30 years by nations such as Israel and Great Britain in order to better elucidate the motivating factors and the risks involved in this dynamic.

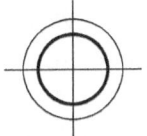

Defining and Explaining Targeted Killing

Discussions pertaining to a national-level policy of premeditated killing of suspected or known terrorists have been hampered historically by the lack of accurate and agreed on definitions of this type of policy. Terms such as 'extrajudicial killing', 'extrajudicial punishment', 'selective targeting', 'assassination policy', 'named killing', and even 'long-range hot pursuit' have been used to describe this specific type of activity.[1] While some of these terms may have partial merit, others serve only to confuse the discussion and hinder debate.

For the purposes of this book, the author adopts the term 'targeted killing' for the following reasons: first and most importantly, this type of offensive counterterrorism action frequently elicits emotional and subjective reactions in the public at large[2], which can result in more pejorative designations, effectively hindering rational and unbiased discussion of the topic. Second, targeted killing is not equivalent to assassination—a term frequently and mistakenly applied to targeted killing—and thus to equate the two results is a misnomer that, again, hampers the discussion.

The author defines targeted killing as: the premeditated, preemptive, and intentional killing of an individual or individuals known or believed to represent a present and/or future threat to the safety and security of a state through affiliation with terrorist groups or individuals. The latter portion of this definition is of particular importance, because the unique nature of terrorism provides states with the specific rationale for the implementation of a policy of targeted killing.

Targeted killings, whether conducted by Israel, the United States, Great Britain, or other nations, are more frequently the result of action undertaken not by conventional military forces, but rather by specialized troops, such as special operations forces (SOF), police, and intelligence agents, as discussed in greater detail below. Alternately, some nations have turned increasingly to specialized equipment, such as unmanned aerial vehicles (UAV) in order to stalk their prey. These specialized troops and equipment have proven to be an essential component of targeted killing, due primarily to the elusive and clandestine nature of terrorists themselves.[3]

Rather than operating from fixed bases, terrorists often use the basements of homes, rented apartments, caves, nomadic encampments, and other locations from which they conduct their planning and subsequent attacks. Moreover, their travel is often concealed, as they do not move about in marked military personnel carriers, but rather in civilian vehicles that are nearly impossible to distinguish. In response to the tactics, conventional weapons of war such as tanks and heavy bombers are all but useless. This type of warfare requires a combination of accurate intelligence, highly trained and specialized soldiers, and oftentimes the use of unique and advanced tracking and detection equipment. Such is the nature of targeted killing.

It is for these reasons, and those cited in later sections of this book, that targeted killing has become a preferred, although inherently limited, method of reducing the threat of terrorism - particularly that posed by specific individuals. While defining this action and providing its basic operational methodologies are relatively simple undertakings, the implementation of this action by the state must also be justified at a governmental level, and to define and agree to such a course of action is a complex undertaking.

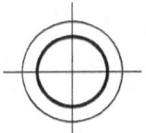

Targeted Killing versus Assassination

Before proceeding with an examination of targeted killing as a method of state self-defence in the war on terrorism, it is important to differentiate between targeted killing and assassination. This is an important distinction in the context of this discussion for two primary reasons: to clearly illuminate the differences between the two, and secondly, to demonstrate that targeted killing is not a method for expressing political or ideological differences, but rather a purely defensive act intended to protect the state and its populace.

Though numerous scholars and other experts have tried, the concept and practice of assassination has proven a complicated concept to define.[4] Decades of research and the resultant books and papers have failed to result in comprehensive and shared parameters and characteristics for this complex concept. For purposes of this discussion, assassination is defined as the premeditated killing of a prominent person for political or ideological reasons.

Assassination, as a political tool, was long considered an acceptable and rational action. As a method of statecraft, it dates back to the earliest recorded governments and includes the death of Julius Caesar in March 44 B.C. Since that time, individuals, groups, and states have participated in the killings of prominent persons (usually heads of state or senior government officials) in order to further their own political or ideological goals. One notable government body was, in fact, based on the concept of assassination. The Ismalian sect founded by Hasan ibn-al-Sabbah had, as its primary function, assassination. Indeed, it has long been believed that we derive the term 'assassination' in use today from the 'assassins'—the *Hashashi* of this sect, though the validity of this belief is currently under debate.[5] [6]

The practice of assassination was long used as a method of expediting political or ideological goals is, as mentioned, a matter of historical fact. What is also equally clear is that assassination, as we term it here, has not been used to preemptively eliminate an individual who planned, personally or as part of a larger group, to asymmetrically attack a given state.[7] Instead, this particular type of killing is reserved for the elimination of political and ideological opponents of prominence.

Despite this background, assassination is today considered a politically and morally unacceptable activity, and has fallen into disuse as a tool in the statecraft of modern nations, though formal steps to renounce its use came about only in the latter half of the 20th century.[8] [9] Even the U.S., which formally outlawed political assassination in 1970 with the signing of Executive Order 12333, was not above employing such tactics, particularly during the Cold War.[10] [11] [12]

We are able to draw a distinct line between assassination and targeted killing. In sum, assassination is the killing of an individual or group of individuals for purely political or ideological reasons. Targeted killing, in contrast, is the killing of an individual or group of individuals without regard for politics or ideology, but rather *exclusively* for reasons of state self-defence.

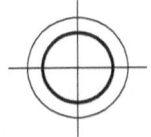

The Norm of Self-Defence

The norm of self-defence may (in its simplest and most basic form) be said to be the right of a sovereign nation to defend itself from internal and external aggression. Self-defence in its truest sense is, of course, the right of *every* nation, none of whom are bound to United Nations Security Council (UNSC) approval in order to exercise this right. In the most basic example, if a nation is invaded by a neighbour, it has the right to use force to repel that invasion. It need not wait until it has pleaded its case to the UN and received Security Council approval to do so. Such a requirement would violate a basic tenet of sovereignty.

This simple example is not intended to suggest that self-defence is not a complex issue, with many different components and arguments relating to its implementation. Innumerable books, articles, papers, and dissertations have been written describing and assessing the various conditions and limits of this norm.

For example, as highlighted in David Rodin's *War & Self-Defence*, there is a difference in the culpability of the aggressor and the innocence of the defender.[13] There is also the issue of historical background, such as in the case of lands taken from a people by force, who then later rise up to reclaim it.[14] The question then arises: who is the aggressor and who is the defender? As stated in the introduction, this book does not seek to answer these broader questions of the norm of self-defence, but rather seeks to clarify whether targeted killing is a justified form of self-defence, and under which conditions it may be employed.

In this international world in which sovereign nations endeavor to exist peacefully despite border disputes, fragile treaties, political differences, and other dynamics, self-defence sometimes becomes not a mere matter of black and white, as suggested in the initial example, but rather a complex, multi-layered consideration. The UN was formed, in part, to untangle this web and to give nations a forum in which to air grievances and settle disputes peacefully. As history has shown, this effort has proven successful in some cases, less successful in others.

In the latter half of the 20th century, and into the 21st century, it has become evident that terrorism, particularly conducted by non-state actors employing transnational terrorism (that is to say without respect for national borders), has become commonplace. Thus, the traditional methods of warfare and self-defence have been thrust into disarray and challenged to their core. States have largely responded to this threat on an individual level, choosing to react to the threat in their own particular ways, while citing their right to self-defence. In some cases, and increasingly so following the attacks of 9/11 and the resulting actions of the U.S., this has meant an escalation in instances of military preemption—attacking before the terrorists themselves can strike.

Needless to say, this proactive approach to countering terrorism has resulted in no small number of instances in which states have found themselves up against the previously solid walls of national sovereignty. As terrorists established safe-havens in Afghanistan during the 1990s, for example, the U.S. has chosen to launch missile strikes against bases there in an effort to kill the terrorists it believed, or knew to be, planning attacks against it.[15] There was little political fallout from these attacks, as nations began to realize that the new terrorist threat, particularly that posed by Islamic extremists, differed greatly from the domestic threats historically posed by the Irish Republican Army (IRA) in the UK, Basque Fatherland and Liberty (ETA) in Spain, and the Revolutionary Armed Forces of Colombia (FARC), who typically stayed within the geographic area in which they had their primary grievances.

This is not to say that states did not recognize the threats posed by terrorists operating regionally. For example, the best-known case of targeted killing, the Israeli pursuit of Black September terrorists following the 1972 Munich Olympics, occurred throughout Europe and the Middle East (see later case study for further details). Thus, there is ample evidence that in some of these cases, states chose to operate in violation of other states' sovereignty in order to conduct reprisals or to otherwise eliminate perceived terrorist threats.

Self-defence and preemption, while perhaps less controversial now than in times past, remains a vociferous subject of international debate. And this debate rises to one of its most heated levels when discussing the practice of targeted killing. Nonetheless, this practice remains at the forefront of the counterterrorist actions of nations such as the U.S., Israel, Russia, and, until recently, Great Britain.

The inherent nature of transnational terrorism precludes much of what may have previously proven effective against conventional enemies in wars past, such as tanks, massed ground forces, and artillery barrages.

Today, the threat hides in cities, mountains, slums, refugee camps, and caves—virtually anywhere it can find a safe haven from which to operate. Therefore, these conventional tools are largely an anachronism (save the unique case of Afghanistan). The rise of targeted killing, then, comes as little surprise due to its specific nature of limiting offensive action to those individuals and locations in which the enemy can be found and engaged.

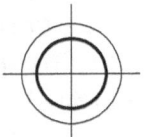

The United Nations, Self-Defence, and Preemption

The right of a nation to take action to defend itself is spelled out in Article 51 of the United Nations Charter, which states:

> Nothing in the present Charter shall impair the inherent right of individual or collective self-defence if an armed attack occurs against a Member of the United Nations, until the Security Council has taken measures necessary to maintain international peace and security. Measures taken by Members in the exercise of this right of self-defence shall be immediately reported to the Security Council and shall not in any way affect the authority and responsibility of the Security Council under the present Charter to take at any time such action as it deems necessary in order to maintain or restore international peace and security.[16]

Many nations have cited Article 51 as a basis for their primary right to undertake unilateral military actions, citing the requirement of self-defence, with or without UN approval. This has, in some cases, worked out well for the acting state (resulting in little or no argument in the UN), yet in some cases, as with the Israeli attack on Iraq, resulted in international condemnation.

Targeted killing is, without question, a form of preemption. Its goal is to proactively eliminate terrorists before they have a chance to inflict harm on the affected state's citizens and/or homeland. However, in many cases of preemption, the states undertaking this action have not sought or been granted authority to do so under the auspices (or even with the sanction of) of the UNSC, and thus the action may be viewed as illegal.[17] For this reason, states taking part in a program of targeted killing against a terrorist threat risk political capital and international prestige when taking such unilateral action.

This type of 'anticipatory self-defence' has taken many forms over the years, such as Israel's strike against Arab targets in the opening hours of the Six Day War in 1967.[18] [19] While a conventional attack (as opposed to asymmetric) and unrelated to terrorism, it is clear that ample evidence existed to convince Israel that a wide scale invasion was imminent and that it needed to strike first in order to survive the expected conflict.[20] While undertaken without UN authorization, the negative political consequences of this action were few, due to the obvious nature of the pending threat.

Israel was not so lucky in 1981, when it unilaterally bombed Iraq's Osirak nuclear reactor complex, which it claimed was being used to create nuclear weapons for use against Israel. Following the attack, the UN Security

Council unanimously adopted a highly critical resolution, followed by an even more strongly worded resolution that appeared tantamount to a threat against Israel, should it repeat its attack.[21][22] Thus, while Israel may have eliminated a potential future threat, it suffered greatly for its actions in the court of world opinion.

So, it appears clear that the concept of self-defence, even as defined in Article 51 is a flexible and debatable concept. As Thomas Frank astutely concludes in *Recourse to Force*:

> When the facts and their political content are widely seen to warrant a pre-emptive or deterrent intervention on behalf of credibly endangered citizens abroad, and if the UN itself, for political reasons, is incapable of acting, then some use of force by a state may be accepted as legitimate self defence with the meaning of Article 51.[23]

The recourse to targeted killing (in itself, preemption), then, may be viewed as a legitimate self-defence in the war against terrorism. As the threat is often transnational and asymmetric, the UN is institutionally and materially ill equipped to deal with each terrorist threat as it arises and spreads. Thus, nations are largely left on their own to resolve the problem.

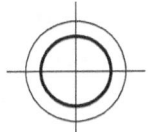

Targeted Killing and Conventional Warfare

One distinction that must be made is that between the use of targeted killing in conventional warfare, with its inherent restrictions as found in the Geneva Conventions, and that of asymmetric warfare. Tradition and the unwritten military code of conduct on the battlefield, too, played a role in restricting the specific targeting of individuals, at least for a period of time.

For example, the tacit prohibition of the intentional and specific killing of generals and other senior officers in wartime is largely a result of historical precedent in which a sort of gentlemen's agreement existed whereby such activity was considered uncivilized.[24] This is not to say, however, that such killings did not occur. During the 1700's and 1800's, sharpshooters on opposing military vessels often targeted officers in order to disrupt command and control and to lower enemy morale.[25]

There is also evidence that the presence of a particular officer in battle may have merited special attention from the enemy. For example, during the battle of Trafalgar in

1805, British Admiral Lord Horatio Nelson was felled by a sniper's bullet. There can be little doubt that the French marksman in that incident was aware that he was targeting Nelson, due not in the least to the distinctive uniforms worn by officers on both sides during the battle.[26]

More to the point, however, is the decision by which a nation's political or military leaders targets a specific individual of the opposing military forces. The goal of such an action is, ostensibly, to remove an officer of such high regard that his death would constitute a significant degradation of enemy warfighting capability: a perfectly legal and acceptable action in the conduct of warfare: provided such actions are taken openly and not through the use of what the Geneva Conventions describe as 'perfidy', as described below.

Examples of a state choosing to target an individual military commander include (but are certainly not limited to) the failed British attempt to kill German Field Marshal Irwin Rommel during the North African campaign, the successful British-Czech plot to kill SS Obergurppenführer Reinhard Heydrich in 1942, and, more recently, U.S. efforts to eliminate Saddam Hussein and his sons during the early days of Operation Iraqi Freedom. [27] [28] [29]

A valuable case study in this context is that of the purposeful and premeditated killing of Japanese Admiral Isoruku Yamamoto during World War II. In April 1943, American code breakers intercepted a message indicating that Admiral Yamamoto would be traveling by air between military bases in the South Pacific. News of this movement was immediately sent to the highest echelons of military and civilian leadership, and a mission specifically intended to kill the admiral was approved.[30] On April 18, 1943, American fighter planes intercepted a flight of Japanese military aircraft transporting Yamamoto to a nearby Japanese base. In the ensuing engagement, Yamamoto's aircraft was shot down and the admiral was killed.

One could make the case that the premeditated killing of Yamamoto and the other cases cited here constitute evidence of targeted killing. If we are to argue that targeted killing is the 'premeditated, preemptive, and deliberate killing of an individual or individuals known to represent a clear and present threat to the safety and security of a state', then perhaps such an argument might have some merit. This is not the case, however. If we put considerations of terrorism aside for the moment, it is evident that military leaders, being part of a military at war, are valid and legitimate targets, the killing of whom is justified under the laws of war.

What is important here is the manner in which the killing is attempted. The 1977 protocol to the Geneva Convention specifically forbids the use of 'perfidy', such as masquerading as a civilian or as a representative of a neutral party (such as the Red Cross).[31] In this case, if a soldier used such methods in order to gain proximity to a given target, he would be in violation of the Geneva Convention and (ostensibly) prosecutable under international law as a war criminal.

By way of example, the plan to kill General Rommel involved the use of commandos who, infiltrated behind enemy lines via submarine and using other methods of operational subterfuge, operated largely within the boundaries of the Convention, to include wearing Allied military uniforms. However, the killers of Obergurppenführer Heydrich in 1942 took a much different approach, wearing civilian clothes and operating outside the parameters of accepted military conduct.[32]

Thus, we can see that the targeting of military leaders of an opposing armed force while in a state of war is a legally acceptable action, and does not represent an example of targeted killing. But what happens when the leader of a given state is deemed responsible for harboring terrorists, or sponsors their nefarious activities?

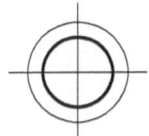

Self-Defence and Targeting State Leaders

As argued previously, the targeting of prominent individuals, such as heads of state, clearly falls under the rubric of assassination. However, one could argue that when that official has direct involvement with and is supportive of a terrorist organization, then his protected status should be called into question—and becomes even more pertinent if that official wears the rank of a military officer. States are clearly responsible for making distinctions between assassination of heads of state and the targeted killing of terrorists, though the issue is, at best, a murky one.

Israel, for example, consistently vacillated on its position as to the targeted killing of Yassir Arafat. Citing his ongoing guidance of and support for Palestinian terrorism, Israeli leaders frequently named Arafat as a legitimate target. Prior to his death, Israeli Prime Minister Ariel Sharon assured President George Bush that he would not kill Arafat. This assurance was reportedly later withdrawn.[33] Ultimately, for reasons unknown, Israel did not undertake such an operation.

Another case study of interest is that of the U.S. attack on Libya in 1986. Following the bombing of the La Belle disco in Germany, the U.S. conducted a unilateral (though with some British support) bombing attack against Libya, code-named Operation El Dorado Canyon. This punitive action targeted various locations, including terrorist training facilities, airfields, air defense networks, and related structures.[34] Accordingly, the majority of targets chosen were linked to known or suspected terrorist activities. One of the targets selected, however, included one of the five personal residences of Libyan president Muhammar Khadafi. Though the presence of his home was known to planners, there is no evidence to indicate that Khadafi himself was intentionally targeted; however, nor was there any effort made to remove the residence from the list.

The ensuing attack resulted in the destruction of numerous facilities (including the Khadafi residence in which his eighteen month-old adopted daughter was killed), aircraft, vehicles, ships, and an estimated 80 soldiers.[35] In the years following the raid, Libyan support for terrorism waned and eventually disappeared. The U.S. and Libya have discussed the removal of Libya from the list of state sponsors of terrorism.[36] Some scholars and authors have argued that the raid on Libya directly influenced Khadafi to opt out of the terrorist business.[37]

While the factual argument could be made that the leader of a state might justifiably be considered a viable option for targeted killing, it is highly unlikely that any state would proceed with such an action without careful consideration. Such a decision might force the state to withstand the likely perception that it has embarked on a state-sponsored assassination—and risk becoming an international pariah.

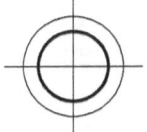

Counterterrorism and Conventional Warfare

Targeted killing is not the killing of a terrorist during routine military or security operations, such as bombing a suspected terrorist camp simply to deny its use by extremists, or raiding a suspected safe house in which unknown terrorists may be located. Targeted killing, for the purposes of this book, is limited to the specific selection of an individual or individuals, who are then tracked down and intentionally killed due to their specific involvement in a terrorist group or action.

This is not to say that a targeted killing cannot occur as part of a larger operation. The scope of the targeted action need not be limited to a strike on a single vehicle, for example. Such was the case with U.S. air operations in Afghanistan following the terrorist attacks of 9/11; a targeted killing (or an attempt at targeted killing) may be conducted as part of a coordinated offensive against a larger enemy (e.g. the Taliban). Such an attempt took place on October 7, 2001, when U.S. warplanes bombed the residence of Mullah Omar, leader of the Taliban. While this attack did not succeed in eliminating its target, it does provide a clear example of a state incorporating targeted killing into a larger overall military campaign.

Additionally, given the dynamic nature of counterterrorist operations, and even during conventional operations, there are occasions when intelligence is uncovered which may lead to the location of a named, wanted terrorist. Tactical intelligence data surfacing in a larger military engagement may present important opportunities for a coordinated targeted killing operation. This can occur in virtually any larger military operation targeting terrorists, such as was often demonstrated during the U.S. campaign in Afghanistan. It comes as no surprise, therefore that a targeted killing operation may, on occasion, arise as a hastily coordinated effort stemming from a much larger military engagement.

Thus, we can see that the death of a terrorist (even a wanted and named terrorist) that occurs coincidentally during the course of a military offensive or operation cannot be termed 'targeted killing.' If intelligence is uncovered, however, during such an action, then a targeted killing may be instigated and acted upon even while that offensive is underway.

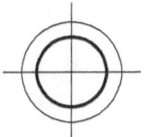

Considering Weapons of Mass Destruction (WMD)

Weapons of mass destruction, also known as WMD, pose potentially the greatest risk of creating massive casualties in the event of a terrorist attack. These weapons (to include the compounds or agents that comprise the lethal component of the same) are generally considered in the following four categories:

1. Nuclear (stolen nuclear warheads, 'suitcase nukes', etc.)
2. Radiological ('dirty bombs')[38]
3. Biological (Anthrax, botulinum toxin, plague, smallpox, etc.)[39]
4. Chemical (biotoxins, blister agents/vesicants, nerve agents, etc.)[40]

Any one of these four categories of weapons brings with it the possibility of a catastrophic level of casualties, depending, of course, on the wide variety of variables inherent in the type, method of delivery, location, and other critical aspects of employment. Thus, potentially, targeted killing becomes an exponentially more important consideration when assessing whether a given terrorist or terrorists are, at any level, pursuing WMD for use in an attack. Individuals who would be likely to rise to the top of the list as candidates for targeted killing in this regard include (in no particular order of importance):

1. Scientists providing technical expertise in the production or construction/weaponization of WMD devices or compounds;
2. Terrorists known to be actively seeking to obtain WMD;
3. Terrorists known to be in possession of WMD;
4. Sympathetic logisticians or supporters working on behalf of a terrorist group to procure WMD.

Obligated to protect its citizens, a state must now consider the new threats posed by terrorists who may be, or actually are, in possession of WMD, in a light perhaps not previously considered by states expecting more conventional threats. In such cases—where a state may know or believe that terrorists are in possession of WMD and planning an attack involving these devices—the motivation and incentive to conduct a targeted killing will understandably become a greater priority.

According to Walter Laquer, in *The New Terrorism: Fanaticism and the Arms of Mass Destruction*, the threat posed by these weapons has heralded an entirely new dynamic with regard to the terrorist threat:

For the first time in history, weapons of enormous destructive power are both readily acquired and harder to track. In this new age, even the cost of hundreds of lives may appear small in retrospect… there is as much fanaticism and madness as there ever was, and there are now very powerful weapons of mass destruction available to the terrorist.[41]

Also to be considered in this category are the related threats posed by terrorists who may seek to strike at nuclear power plants or chemical facilities in order to release radioactive gasses or toxic clouds to cause mass casualties. Following 9/11, numerous U.S. government agencies concluded that American nuclear power plants were indeed vulnerable to such attacks, and suggested steps to increase security.[42] These concerns are not new, of course, but these concerns must not be excluded from any discussion of the terrorist threat to such facilities.[43]

These latter threats are included here specifically to highlight the threat that may be posed by a single individual or a small group of individuals who, while not in possession of WMD, may cause mass casualties due to the nature of their target. In short, terrorists need not bear WMD in order to represent a threat equal to the use of WMD.

It may be said, then, that states should be more inclined to consider offensive, pre-emptive actions in order to counter these new terrorist threats. To rely on previously sufficient or accepted modes of 'counterterrorism' or 'antiterrorism' may expose the state to a level of risk not previously understood or appreciated.[44] Therefore, we can see that it is possible that states may come to consider or even rely on targeted killing as an accepted form of preemption, or, in fact, realize that it may have no alternative than to resort to this course of action, even if such a consideration was once anathema to the national consensus and consciousness against such a practice.

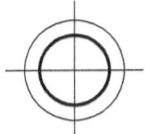

Who Conducts Targeted Killings?

Due to the fact that targeted killings are largely carried out in the utmost secrecy, it is difficult to ascribe any single killing to any particular individual, unit, agency, military, or even a given nation. In some cases, such as attacks on Palestinian extremists in the Gaza Strip, the perpetrator is almost exclusively Israel, which is often ascribed responsibility for such incidents.[45] But whom, then, does Israel call on to carry out such actions? An examination of this dynamic provides insight into the delicate nature of targeted killing and, for that reason, is warranted here.

Typically, states call on the most secretive elements of their national civilian and military agencies to conduct these operations. In particular, those assigned to such missions are usually drawn from intelligence, special operations, or other elite professions. The reasons for this are obvious: specialized training in reconnaissance, close quarters combat, explosives, communications, and clandestine or covert operations.

It is this latter skill and experience that usually provides states with the most valued component of a targeted killing operation: plausible deniability. Plausible deniability is the specific effort of a state to conceal the nature and relation of the targeted killing team and its action to the sponsoring state. In this way a state can participate in this activity with, ostensibly, little risk that a discovered attack will be attributed to it, thus avoiding possible political repercussions on the world stage or even retaliation from the target's supporters, if any.

Thus, in Israel, these missions are typically assigned to members of the Mossad (responsible for human intelligence collection, counterterrorism, and covert action), Shin Bet (internal security), Aman (military intelligence) or one of a number of highly trained police or military special operations units, such as the elite Sayeret Matkal.[46]

In the U.S., a few select units carry out these types of operations. These include the Central Intelligence Agency's Special Activities Staff (within the Directorate of Operations), the U.S. Army's Delta Force, and the U.S. Navy's Naval Special Warfare Development Group (also known as SEAL Team Six).[47] Other, more conventional units may also be called on, as needed, to conduct such operations (particularly in the event that these more specialized units are not within an acceptable striking distance of a fleeting target of opportunity), though these instances are likely rare.

These units, which have similar counterparts in dozens of other nations, including Russia, France, and Great Britain, are specifically trained to operate clandestinely and covertly, including operating in civilian attire, using false documentation and identities. They are equally proficient in the use of small arms, explosives, and other requisite skills.

It is important to note the nature of these personnel, as their ability to operate without attribution to their sponsor state is of paramount importance in most instances of targeted killing. Unless a state chooses to make public its participation in such actions, that state must possess these requisite skills in order to undertake such missions. Thus, we can see that states without these types of operatives are limited in their abilities, and may not be able to make use of targeted killing without risking national or international exposure, and the problems inherent therein.

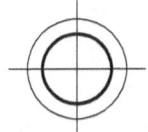

State Study: Israel

For decades, Israel has been the world's leading practitioner of targeted killing. It has consistently cited its need to defend its citizens from the actions of Palestinian terrorists and related threats. This policy has sparked no end of debate, both within Israel and around the world.[48] Nonetheless, it has also resulted in the only known codification of the prerequisites for targeted killing.

In April 2002, Israeli Defence Force (IDF) lawyers set forth the following four conditions for targeted killing[49]:

- There must be well-supported information showing that the terrorist will plan or carry out a terrorist attack in the near future
- The policy can be enacted only after appeals to the Palestinian Authority calling for the terrorist's arrest have been ignored.
- Attempts to arrest the suspect by use of IDF troops have failed.
- The targeted killing is not to be carried out in retribution for events of the past. Instead it can

only be done to prevent attacks in the future which are liable to toll multiple casualties.

In January 2003, former Israeli intelligence officials claimed that Israel had expanded its policy of targeted killing to the discharging of such action in other nations, including the U.S.[50] This assertion was vehemently denied by current Israeli officials, but historical evidence is clear on the fact that Tel Aviv has previously authorized such operations.[51]

However, codified or not, rarely does an instance of targeted killing conducted by the Israelis go without notice or some form of public remonstration. The greatest recent political fallout from Israel's ongoing application of this practice occurred in 2004 with the killing of HAMAS spiritual leader Sheikh Ahmed Yassin.

Case Study: The Killing of HAMAS Spiritual Leader Sheikh Yassin

On March 22, 2004, founder and spiritual leader of the Palestinian terrorist group HAMAS, 67-year-old Sheikh Ahmed Yassin, was killed by guided missiles fired from an Israeli helicopter as he was pushed in his wheelchair from a mosque en route to his vehicle. The killing sparked protests in the Middle East and formal condemnation from nations such as Britain and France.[52] [53]

As the founder of HAMAS, Yassin was an early participant in the planning of terrorist activities. His role in recent years however, at least in the eye of public perception, was primarily that of a spiritual rather than an operational leader. Because much of the world viewed his killing through a religious prism, Israel was placed in the awkward position of justifying the death of an elderly, crippled man who was bound to a wheelchair and unable to take an active role in terrorist attacks.

The political fallout from his death was multiplied because world opinion felt the killing had a negative impact on the ongoing and sensitive Middle East peace process. It was for this reason that the world audience called into question his killing (though this was also due to its negative impact on the sensitive Middle East peace process): how could Israel justify killing an elderly, wheelchair-bound civilian who was obviously not going to be participating in any attacks himself?

From Israel's perspective, given Yassin's continued affiliation with HAMAS—he often blessed those who took part in attacks against Israelis–he clearly represented a terrorist threat and was complicit in their actions. Nonetheless, this answer, when coupled with the widespread media coverage of Yassin in his wheelchair prior to the attack and later photos of the destroyed wheelchair generated widespread criticism and condemnation of Israel in the world community.

In sum, the targeted killing of Yassin is an example of an operation that was technically justifiable and well within the parameters produced by the Israelis, but which was condemned by the international community and which cost Tel Aviv a large amount of political capital.

In February 2005, Israel announced a package of concessions to the Palestinians that included an end to the policy of targeted killings.[54] Whether or not Israel adheres to this decision will depend on the level of future Palestinian terrorist aggression. Should such attacks resume and escalate, it is likely that Israel will opt to resume its policy of targeted killing as an early response.

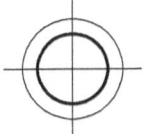

State Study: United States

Prior to 1985, the United States preferred to remain in a reactive posture with regard to international terrorism. Following the hijacking of the Italian cruise liner Achille Lauro by Palestinian terrorists, and the resultant execution of U.S. citizen Leon Klinghoffer, this posture became more forward leaning. According to former Israeli Prime Minister Benjamin Netanyahu, the genesis of this more offensive approach originated, in part, in a series of discussions between Netanyahu and then-Secretary of State George Shultz.[55] In a 1985 speech at the Jonathan Institute, Shultz stated:

> Can we as a country, can the community of free nations, stand in a purely defensive posture and absorb the blows dealt by terrorists? I think not. From a practical standpoint, a purely passive defence does not provide enough of a deterrent to terrorism and the states that sponsor it. It is time to think long, hard, and seriously about more active means of defence – defence through appropriate

preventive or preemptive actions against terrorist groups before they strike.[56]

Following the attacks of September 11, 2001, the Bush Administration was confronted with having to respond, more aggressively than ever before, to the threat of international terrorism.[57] Washington did not wait long, however, before making it clear to the world that a new era of 'anticipatory self-defence' had been ushered in, and that the U.S. would follow this course of action in order to kill or capture terrorists worldwide.[58]

President Bush further outlined this more aggressive, offensive approach to counterterrorism in a speech to the 2002 graduating class at the U.S. Military Academy at West Point:

> Our security will require transforming the military you will lead—a military that must be ready to strike at a moment's notice in any dark corner of the world. And our security will require all Americans to be forward-looking and resolute, to be ready for preemptive action when necessary to defend our liberty and to defend our lives.[59]

Since that time, the U.S. has conducted innumerable global counterterrorist operations, both successful and unsuccessful targeted killings against such prominent terrorist figures as Osama bin Ladin and Mullah Omar and their key lieutenants.[60] So intent is the U.S. in locating these individuals that it has included many on an official 'wanted' list, which offers multi-million dollar rewards for information leading to their apprehension.[61]

Case Study: The Killing of al-Harithi

The most public example of targeted killing by the U.S. against an individual terrorist occurred on November 3, 2002, when a Predator unmanned aerial vehicle (UAV), armed with Hellfire guided missiles, was used to attack a vehicle in which the terrorist was traveling.[62] The resulting explosion killed all in the vehicle, including the suspected target, Abu Ali al-Harithi, an al Qaeda leader and one of the terrorist network's top figures in Yemen.

Officials in the U.S. still refused to admit responsibility for the attack, though a significant amount of reporting indicates that the Central Intelligence Agency (CIA) operated the drone. The day following the attack, U.S. Secretary of Defence Donald Rumsfeld was asked if the U.S. had been involved in the explosion. He did not identify those responsible for the attack, though he did seem well aware of the target.

The following exchange is insightful and is provided as an example of the plausible deniability with which the U.S. and other nations often approach public questions about incidents of targeted killing.[63]

> Q: Mr. Secretary, what can you tell us about the car explosion that was reported today in Yemen? Were any U.S. forces involved in that? And have you learned anything about the aftermath of who was killed in that event?
>
> Rumsfeld: I've seen the reports. And the discussion in one of the reports–I didn't notice whose report it was, but it looked like a wire service report of something out of the region–it said that Harithi

might be involved, in which case, as I recall, he was in fact one of the people that is thought to have been involved with the USS Cole.

Q: Have you confirmed that through government sources?

Rumsfeld: No. I have not. And needless to say, he has been an individual that has been sought after as an al Qaeda member, as well as a suspected terrorist connected to the USS Cole.[64] So it would be a very good thing if he were out of business.

It is clear that targeted killing has become an accepted American foreign policy option, with a tacit rationale in self-defence. While this undoubtedly will result in questions about its legality and, perhaps more importantly, the volatile issue of the U.S. military conduct of operations abroad, there is little question that this practice will continue.

The policy of targeted killing, as adopted by the U.S., has also caused consternation among legal observers who feel that this method of premeditated killing crosses the boundary set forth in Executive Order 12,333, which bans assassinations. However, it is clear that the U.S. justifies this approach as part of its 'global war on terror', and thus applies the rules of war. Simply put, it argues that terrorists are not civilians, and are in fact enemy combatants, and are thus legitimate targets.

This assessment can be supported when considering that, as both terrorism and counterterrorism are forms of asymmetric—not conventional—warfare, it is difficult to ascribe the same methodologies and judgments that might have been present in World War II. For example, no longer is the enemy wearing distinct uniforms, carrying their weapons openly, or even obeying the *spirit* of the Geneva Convention.

Additionally, given that the 'battlefield' is undefined and that a terrorist attack can occur anywhere, the armed interdiction of a terrorist must sometimes necessarily occur in locations and at times not necessarily preferred or chosen by the authorities. That targeted killings occur is, in some cases, an act of necessity in order to prevent an imminent attack. While this argument will be addressed in full below, it is sufficient here to note that the U.S., like other nations, must necessarily reserve its right to self-defence, particularly against an asymmetric threat such as terrorism.

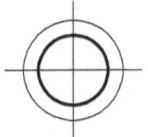

State Study: Great Britain

Great Britain's long history of involvement in Northern Ireland brought with it innumerable challenges in attempting to combat the terrorist threat. These challenges resulted in many changes to British law as it pertains to terrorism, as well as the adaptation of the security and military forces to combat it on the ground. The inclusion of Great Britain in this discussion also serves to highlight the difficulties inherent in justifying targeted killing. Specifically, it clearly presents the challenges present even in the face of what appears to be overwhelming evidence that a targeted killing was undertaken to stop terrorist actions immediately prior to and, in fact, during their execution.

The Loughall case, which we will examine here, also highlights numerous ancillary aspects of targeted killing, namely, the question of an unspoken policy (allegedly in place during the 1970s and 1980s) of 'ambushing' IRA terrorists rather than attempting to effect their arrest, the hazards of targeted killing and collateral damage, and the potential for political backlash in the event of a questionable (or legally challenged) interdiction.

In an effort to provide improved tactical guidance to its military forces in Northern Ireland, the British government mandated the distribution of the 'Yellow Card.' The Yellow Card was, quite literally that: a laminated card to be carried at all times by British military personnel. On the card were the official guidelines for the use of force by British soldiers.

Among the general rules were (selected rules provided verbatim)[65]:

- Never use more force than the minimum necessary to enable you to carry out your duties.
- If you have to challenge a person who is acting suspiciously you must do so in a firm, distinct, voice saying 'HALT – HANDS UP.'
- If the person does not halt at once, you are to challenge again saying 'HALT-HANDS UP' and, if the person does not halt on your second challenge, you are to cock your weapon, apply the safety catch, and shout, 'STAND STILL I AM READY TO FIRE.'

Of course, the soldier could not simply engage any individual he wished, Yellow Card or not. He had to have reasonable cause, such as the perception of a legitimate threat to himself or his fellow soldiers.

Mark Urban offers in his book *Big Boys Rules* that as the term 'ambush' was often used by officers briefing their men prior to a counterterrorist operation, and that the Yellow Card was thus often disregarded, such is evidenced in this interview between Urban and an SAS member:[66]

URBAN: What is the mission on an ambush?

SAS MAN: You know what the mission is on an ambush, everybody knows what the mission is on an ambush.

URBAN: Tell me what you think it is.

SAS MAN: I know that when you do an ambush you kill people.

Case study: Loughall, Northern Ireland.
In May 1987, British intelligence units began monitoring several well-known and active IRA terrorists who were planning an attack against a Royal Ulster Constabulary (RUC) station in Loughall, Northern Ireland.[67] In anticipation, both the SAS and police surveillance experts worked out a coordinated effort to monitor the terrorists for days prior to the expected attack. Authorities also staked out the location where the explosives to be used in the attack were located, a farmhouse located just kilometers from the RUC station.

On the day of the planned bombing, the two terrorists were joined by six other group members who approached the station in a van and a stolen tractor, to which had been affixed a massive 200-pound explosive device. The terrorists planned to drive the tractor into the RUC compound and detonate the device, thus leveling the station. After the attack, they would steal any weapons in the station, then beat a hasty retreat.[68]

At least 50 armed military and police personnel (including additional SAS personnel flown into Northern Ireland specifically for this action) had taken up hidden positions around the area in order to interdict the terrorists. In an interesting twist, the SAS also posted men inside the station, despite the assessment that the station itself was the target. The mission briefing described the operation as a 'massive ambush.'[69]

Unaware of the presence of the authorities and the impending ambush, the terrorists arrived, alighted their vehicle, and opened fire on the station. At the same time, the tractor was driven up to the gate of the compound, where the terrorists lit the fuse to detonate the device, which exploded and partially destroyed the station. As they opened fire, however, the combined SAS/police force reacted, firing an estimate 1,200 rounds at the gunmen.[70] All IRA personnel were killed in the ensuing gun battle, as was one civilian, who happened to be driving through the area at the time of the ambush.

While it may be argued that this incident was a clear case of self-defence, the European High Court in 1991 ruled against the UK, citing violations of the human rights of the eight dead terrorists.[71] While the court did not rule the shootings illegal, they did determine that the ensuing investigation conducted by the British government was in violation due to what the court deemed 'faulty effectiveness of investigation into shooting.'[72] This result demonstrates, again, the political risks states run in conducting what may be a justifiable case of targeted killing.

Additionally, it appears that there can be no argument that the force sent to interdict the terrorists in this case was intentionally placed in that position not to arrest them, but rather to kill them. Had the authorities wished to simply arrest the eight men, this could have been accomplished in the days preceding the attack.[73] Thus, despite denials by the British military and legal challenges brought to the European High Court, the Loughall incident appears to be a textbook case of targeted killing.

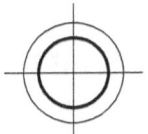

When is Targeted Killing Justified?

While this book avoids ascribing moral or ethical judgments to this discussion of targeted killing, it is of value to examine the circumstances in which states can legitimately claim that the use of targeted killing is within the norm of self-defence. In any offensive lethal action, there exist any number of opportunities for accidents and abuse. As mentioned above, there are no universally accepted laws governing the use of targeted killing. Each nation is responsible for applying its own domestic laws and concepts of self-defence when considering this option. In the absence of actual laws, therefore, it may be beneficial to examine a hypothetical scenario in which targeted killing might be justified as self-defence.

For example, if a terrorist were observed packing a vehicle with explosives, wiring the explosives to a handheld detonator, then driving that vehicle towards a crowd of soldiers or a crowded marketplace (or a police station, in the case of the Loughall incident described above), it seems reasonable to assume that eliminating that terrorist would be justified. In this case, it would appear that there could be little argument against the idea that a terrorist who is in the process of carrying out a terrorist attack is a legitimate subject for targeted killing.[74] The duty of a state to protect its citizens from this threat is clear and unassailable, and the terrorist's death (assuming for the sake of argument that he could not be captured alive) is a necessary outcome.

This example of a terrorist in action is the exception to the rule, of course. Many times, targeted killings take place far from the scene of an attack, both in time and place. For example, in the case of the U.S. targeted killing of al-Harithi, his detection and interdiction took place two years and hundreds of miles away from the act for which the U.S. held him accountable: the attack on the USS Cole. In this case, the U.S. cited al-Harithi's ongoing and active membership in al Qaeda as the basis for his killing.

So, we can see that the dynamics of international terrorism severely test the one truly effective countermeasure that is able to combat it: targeted killing. Just as there is no universally accepted definition of the term, there is equally no universally accepted norm under which its use is permitted, even in what might seem the most direct cases of state self-defence.

As mentioned previously, killings conducted for political reasons rather than for direct security concerns are not targeted killing, but rather assassinations. For example, as cited in the case of Israel's elimination of Sheikh Ahmed Yassin, there are individuals whose elimination may serve both purposes. The death of Yassin both eliminated a high-ranking politico-religious figure, and it may also have had a negative effect on HAMAS' ability to wage its terrorist campaign.

However, within the world of terrorism and insurgency, it is often difficult to differentiate between those participating in terrorism directly, and those providing political, moral, or spiritual leadership. Very often, these are intertwined. In these instances, nations can be expected to mould and modify their explanations for a given killing to fit the circumstances (particularly to avoid either a domestic or international political backlash). For example, Russia's killing of senior Chechen military leaders may, on one hand, be justified in that they are indeed in command of troops in the field. On the other hand, they are also serving in senior political positions. This dual responsibility often provides the aggressor state with justification for eliminating political leaders under the pretext of eliminating a terrorist threat.

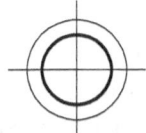

Targeted Killing at the Strategic, Operational, and Tactical Levels

It is difficult to determine at what stages and with what results targeted killing may be considered to have 'worked.' The value placed on the success of such a mission is wholly dependent on the expected outcome. Do the aggressors intend, with such a killing, to bring about the collapse of a given group? Or, are the goals less grand, simply with the intention of preventing a specific attack?

The answer may be more internalized, rooted in the motivations and methodologies of the terrorist group itself. Does the group seek death as part of its operational repertoire, or even as the means to an end, such as in the case of martyrdom? Or, does it endeavor to keep its operatives alive, so as to fight another day? There are three areas which must be considered here in order to fully answer this question: strategic, operational, and tactical. These issues are critical when determining whether a targeted killing can even possibly be considered successful.

Strategic

In answering the first series of questions, the preponderance of information leads to the conclusion that the targeted killing of senior leaders or individuals does not lead to the dissolution or usually even a severe degradation of that group's capabilities or intentions. This is particularly true in the case of those groups with long, established histories and large or highly motivated memberships, or a wide support base (e.g. al Qaeda, the Revolutionary Armed Forces of Colombia [FARC], or Spain's ETA). These include terrorist groups, for example, that are seeking national identity.[75] Smaller groups, such as the Red Army Faction and the Red Brigades survived the killing and imprisonment of key leaders and continued operations for years.

To borrow a conclusion from senior RAND terrorism analyst Brian Jenkins in his commentary in *Newsday* (December 3, 2003):

> The more an enterprise draws from deep roots or has a broad base, the less the effect of the death of its leader. It is not the loss of a single leader that fells a movement, but the elimination of its leadership, operational capabilities, constituency and conditions.[76]

Additionally, the elimination (particularly the violent termination) of a leader, who has gained a 'mythic' status amongst his supporters, can serve to demoralize a terrorist movement. As this mythic quality can often serve as a force multiplier in a terrorist campaign, the elimination of this element can have a strong impact. This is particularly true if the leader has previously identified himself (or is perceived by followers) to be immune to capture or death at the hands of the enemy.

Yet, these considerations do not wholly limit the potential effectiveness or applicability of targeted killing. It is likely that less established, newly founded groups may be more susceptible to such actions. This is an important consideration when states are confronted, for example, with the phenomenon of splinter groups—smaller, usually more violent offshoots of larger, more established (and oftentimes more politically reasonable) terrorist groups. As such, splinter groups are inherently (as least in their nascent stages) not as well supported as their parent body. They are more vulnerable to eradication through the arrest or the killing of their ostensibly more radical leaders.

This is to say that such groups are typically less well financed, less well supported, and more reliant on an individual or a small group for their moral guidance and operational viability. Thus, this critical node of the splinter group is a key element (likely *the* essential element) in its existence, the removal of which would likely result in its deformation and eventual dissipation.

Another, possibly more important aspect of the debate surrounding targeted killing is that it may serve as a viable tool in strategic efforts to reduce terrorism. The difference here lies not in the target selection, *per se*, but rather in the motivations and beliefs of the targeted group itself. Within those terrorist groups whose goal is not martyrdom, but rather survival (e.g. IRA volunteers), the effects of targeted killing are much different. While Islamic extremist terrorists may seek death as a way to enter a desirable religious afterlife, and thus are not deterred by the deaths of comrades by whatever means, this is not the case with many secular groups, or groups who do not share a given belief system.

Thus, while targeted killing may not prove a disincentive to those former groups, the reality is much different among groups who seek to survive their attacks and 'live to fight another day.' This difference may also complicate the efforts of those groups seeking to survive and flourish in the long run. For example, according to one former British SAS veteran with 20 years' experience in Northern Ireland and in other conflicts, the killing of group members, particularly leaders, had a decisively negative impact on future recruiting efforts.[77] It is also possible that such elements that may be present among secular terrorists, such as the quite understandable fear of being killed, may also prove a strong disincentive in the face of a (either overt or covert) targeted killing campaign.

Operational

In an operational sense, the selective elimination of key personnel, particularly those with critical skills (i.e. bomb makers, logisticians, recruiters, financiers), is likely to have a detrimental effect on the short to mid-term operations of any terrorist group. Certainly, the larger the group, the less the impact, due to the probability of a group being able to replace that individual—or to shift another, equally qualified individual into the role of the displaced member.

Additionally, and particularly in the case of Islamic extremism, the sheer volume of potential recruits greatly reduces the overall operational impact of targeted killing. As the daily occurrence of suicide bombings in nations around the world proves, despite the number of terrorists killed in such attacks, the supply of candidates for the next day's attacks appears limitless. This, too, affects not only the operational perspectives on targeted killing, but that of its strategic questions as well. In an environment in which the targets are ostensibly perpetual, can targeted killing truly have an impact to a significant enough level to justify its risks?

It may be argued that, when faced with a seemingly constant influx of suicide volunteers, states must nonetheless act to interdict these individuals when and where they appear, to both interrupt the flow of new recruits and to (ostensibly) preclude future attacks. The idea of inaction against such a known threat is unthinkable in a modern state. Thus, while targeted killing has only a limited impact on some terrorist groups, it is a necessary and logical tool for use in preventing future attacks. Much like the multitude of hapless soldiers who swarmed up out of the trenches into the face of machine gun fire in World War I, the enemy had to be engaged, lest they overrun friendly forces and gain territory.

In fact, while this assessment is partly based on the author's analysis, it may be that targeted killing serves as an operational deterrent to terrorism. With the practice, at least as conducted by the U.S. and Israel, well known to civilians and terrorists alike, it is possible and even likely that this knowledge may force terrorists to operate in a more clandestine mode, thus hindering their operational capabilities, perhaps even reducing the number of attacks.

In some cases, even the threat of targeted killing may be sufficient to produce a positive result (i.e. the release of hostages). One example of this occurred in June 1985, when Shiite terrorists hijacked a TWA flight en route from

Athens to Rome. The plane was then diverted to Beirut, Lebanon. There, the terrorists tortured several passengers, eventually executing one U.S. Navy diver and tossing his body onto the tarmac, in plain sight of international news crews.

In the days that followed, the terrorists removed the hostages from the plane and dispersed them throughout Beirut, in an effort to complicate any possible armed rescue attempt.

According to an account by former Israeli Prime Minister Benjamin Netanyahu in *Fighting Terrorism*, the office of the U.S. Secretary of State asked his advice as to how they should proceed. Netanyahu responded: "'Issue a counter-threat,' I told him. 'Make it clear to the terrorists that if they so much as touch a hair on any of the hostages' heads, you won't rest until every last one of them has been hunted down and wiped out.'"[78]

The Secretary's office later reported back to Netanyahu that they had acted on his advice and the results had been positive. A few weeks later, all the hostages were released unharmed. While this release was due, in part, to a previously negotiated settlement unrelated to the hijacking and subsequent kidnapping, it is possible that the counter-threat of targeted killing achieved its desired result.

Another, slightly different, example of this potential by-product of targeted killing occurred in December 1975 when two IRA terrorists, quite literally on the run from authorities, barged into an occupied apartment and took two civilian hostages. The incident ended on the sixth day when authorities announced that an SAS team had arrived on scene and was prepared to storm the apartment.[79] In this case, the perceived threat to their lives presented by the presence of the SAS was enough to cause the terrorists to surrender.

It is important to note—there is no evidence to indicate that the intentions of the SAS team at the scene were in any way related to a predetermined course of targeted killing. It must be noted, however, that the *reputation* of the SAS as feared, ruthless killers was widely believed throughout the UK, and particularly in Northern Ireland. This mythology would play itself out over the next decade, when the SAS killed at least 28 IRA members in various confrontations.[80]

Despite these potential and actual benefits, it must be noted that attempting to reduce a group's operational capabilities through targeted killing is of limited utility when posed against groups practicing advanced security measures. In *Inside Al Qaeda*, author Rohan Gunaratna identifies one crucial aspect:

> To ensure al Qaeda's operational effectiveness, the group stresses the need to maintain internal security, dividing its operatives into overt and covert members functioning under a single leader...al Qaeda's global network has survived by its members strictly adhering to the principles of operational security.[81]

The continued 'success' of al Qaeda (measured in its ability to conduct major terrorist attacks worldwide despite international efforts to eradicate it) is a testament to its members' adherence to operational security. More importantly, for purposes of this discussion, this ongoing viability is evidence of the ineffectiveness of targeted killing (as practiced by the U.S. in this case) in providing a significant detriment to the group's operational capabilities.[82]

Tactical

Targeted killing may be said to 'work' in its most obvious sense when it directly results in the thwarting of an imminent terrorist attack; the surveillance and interdiction of known, armed terrorists en route to an airport, or driving a truck laden with explosives towards a city centre, or even a lone, armed terrorist entering a subway system. All of these would likely be considered justifiable killings, and would most certainly be examples (if successfully interdicted) of the effective use of targeted killing. In this, its most elemental form, is found its most immediate and appropriate function.

One example is the SAS killing of three IRA terrorists in Gibraltar in 1988. While this case is an ongoing matter of debate as to whether the SAS soldiers involved intended to kill the IRA terrorists, this provides a concrete example of the efficacy of surveilling and intentionally engaging named terrorists known to be planning an imminent attack.

In early 1988, three known IRA terrorists traveled to Gibraltar with the purpose of planting a large explosive device in a car to target British soldiers during a changing of the guard ceremony at the governor's residence.[83] The SAS team was warned that the device might be detonated by a remote control in the hands of one of the terrorists. To prevent this, British and Spanish intelligence services cooperated in their efforts to surveil the trio as they traveled from Ireland to Gibraltar.

On the afternoon of March 6th, a small SAS team confronted the three and, in the ensuing melee, shot all three dead. The resultant investigation (mandatory in cases of the military's use of lethal force outside a combat zone) revealed that the IRA members were all armed, though there was no bomb in the car (the device was later located in a neighboring town), and the killings were declared legal following a military tribunal. No bystanders and none of the SAS personnel were injured.

Clearly, the actions of the SAS in this case thwarted an imminent attack that almost certainly would have killed and injured numerous British soldiers and visiting tourists. This case, if in fact the order was given to kill the individuals, served to prevent an atrocity that would otherwise have taken place. Thus, in this sense, we have strong indicators that targeted killing can indeed serve as a lawful and proactive measure in combating terrorism.

On the tactical level, targeted killing has its most obvious application: stopping a terrorist before he has the opportunity to conduct an imminent attack. A sovereign state has the duty to act to protect its citizenry, and in cases where a clear and present danger exists, such as in the case of an imminent terrorist attack, targeted killing becomes a more viable option than perhaps in the preceding two categories.

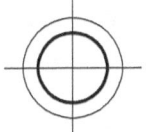

When Does Targeted Killing 'Fail'

As we have seen, targeted killing can have a beneficial impact on several levels for those states waging counterterrorist campaigns. However, it is equally important to analyse the numerous ways in which a policy of targeted killing can backfire and create a host of unforeseen problems for states that engage in this type of action. Among the most important potential weaknesses of targeted killing are the possibilities of collateral damage, creating martyrs, the failure to exploit potential terrorist resources through capture rather than killing, and the possibility of negative international political repercussions.

Collateral Damage

One issue to be considered is clearly that of 'collateral damage'—more specifically, the potential for loss of life among innocent bystanders at the scene of an attack. While the killing of an innocent person directly (such as the Mossad's failed operation in Lillehammer) is indeed quite rare, the nature of terrorists, operating not from fixed bases but rather in virtually any environment, increases the likelihood of civilian exposure.[84] The potential risk is posed to those who may happen to be walking by a booby-trapped vehicle, sitting in an outdoor café next to a wanted terrorist, or merely sauntering down a city street as a missile attack is launched from a nearby helicopter.

Some notable recent examples include the following:

Date	Target	Method	Result
May 30, 2004	Wael Nassar, head of Izzedine al Qassam, Hamas' military wing	Airstrike, Israeli Air Force	Target and bodyguard killed; one civilian killed[85]
March 22, 2004	Sheikh Ahmed Yassin	Airstrike, Israeli Air Force	Target killed; six bystanders killed, numerous injured[86]
June 10, 2003	Abdel Aziz Rantisi, Leader of Gaza-based HAMAS unit	Airstrike, Israeli Air Force	Target escaped; six civilians killed[87]
July 23, 2002	Salah al-Shahada, Hamas military leader	Airstrike, Israeli Air Force	Target killed; 14 civilians killed, 140 injured[88]

October 7, 2001	Mullah Omar, Taliban leader	Airstrike, U.S.	Target absent; two civilians killed[89]
November 9, 2000	Hussein Abayat, Fatah member	Airstrike, Israeli Air Force	Target killed; two civilians killed[90]

There are innumerable other examples like these, though usually involving lower-ranking terrorists. The fallout from collateral damage continues to plague targeted killing operations and draws greater attention to the potential for innocent loss of life. For example, on July 15, 2005, the Israeli Air Force launched a missile attack against a van as it transited a street in Gaza City, killing four HAMAS terrorists, including the bodyguard of a high-ranking group member.[91] The van contained a cache of homemade rockets and explosives, which subsequently detonated, sending shards of fragmentation hundreds of yards in all directions.[92] No bystanders were reported killed or injured, but given the nature of the cargo and the location of the van on a city street, the potential for such casualties was obvious.

The potential risk of injuring or killing bystanders, then, is clear due in no small measure to the elusive nature of the target and the terrorist's proclivity for operating in urban areas or locations otherwise crowded with civilians. Unless the preoperational intelligence is fully accurate and can verify that there are no explosives or other potentially lethal items in the possession of the terrorist, there can be no way to predict the outcome of a violent encounter. Even in the absence of the use of a vehicle, the chaotic results of a missile strike or a booby-trapped car bomb cannot be accurately and definitively predicted. In these and other scenarios, civilians are often inadvertently placed in harm's way due to the dynamic nature of hunting down and killing terrorists, whatever their location.

The Martyrdom Effect

Another potential downside to targeted killing is what, for the purposes of this discussion, is termed the 'martyrdom effect'. This well-known dynamic occurs when a terrorist, particularly one held in high esteem by group members and followers, is killed at the hands of security forces. This can result in the perceptual uplifting of that terrorist to near mythic status, thus inspiring followers to avenge the killing, and thereby fostering an ongoing cycle of violence. While the subject of martyrdom is sufficiently vast to fill tomes, it is beyond the scope of this book to fully address this phenomenon. Its impact on targeted killing, however, necessitates a cursory discussion here.

As detailed above, even if the killing does not result in retributive attacks, it can also serve to increase (not decrease) the morale of a given group. Such events are frequently witnessed following the death of a senior group member and the ensuing mass funeral marches common throughout the Middle East. Billboards throughout the Gaza Strip and elsewhere, for example, extol the sacrifice and bravery of suicide bombers and other terrorists who have met violent ends.

Such is the nature of terrorism today, particularly Islamic extremist terrorism, whereby martyrdom has become not just a by-product of a terrorist act, but *per se* a primary motivation for that act in itself.[93] This phenomenon is unlike the Irish hunger strikers of the 1970s or any of the deaths of secular terrorists in action where martyrdom was not the primary motivation for individual involvement in an action resulting in death. Such was the case with the IRA's Bobby Sands (a hunger striker whose death caused a major outpouring of sympathy and support within the Northern Ireland Republican community and elsewhere). In some cases these deaths did indeed result in their elevation to what may only be described as martyr status.

Thus, we can see that there is an important difference between the 'martyrdom' of a secular terrorist (which arises primarily from respect and acknowledgement of sacrifice for a given action) and that of a religious terrorist (whose martyrdom is accepted as the final reward of his actions from a higher power). That difference is that the secular terrorist desires to live beyond the attack cycle, while the religious terrorist *seeks and expects* his death as part of the attack itself.

Killing versus Capture

Another factor that must be considered is that of the choice made by states to kill rather than capture a known terrorist. In the short term, particularly in instances of an expected imminent attack, targeted killing may be unavoidable to prevent the loss of innocent life. However, in those cases in which a terrorist or terrorists are monitored for long periods of time and do not appear to be involved in a near-term attack, their killing may not only be unnecessary but might also eliminate a potentially valuable source of intelligence.

A good example of this was the arrest of senior al Qaeda planner Khalid Sheikh Mohammad (a/k/a KSM) in March 2003 by Pakistani police officers. It is clear from the evidence that these forces could easily have killed KSM, had they chosen to do so. Instead, recognizing the potentially vast amount of intelligence they could gather from him regarding previous and future planning for terrorist attacks, they opted to arrest rather than kill him. The resulting interrogations revealed valuable insight into al Qaeda and their global network and operations.[94]

Information gleaned from the interrogation of captured terrorists can result in the capture or killing of higher-ranking group leaders, the disruption of attack planning, interdiction of lines of communication, and a host of other related benefits.[95] Therefore, while the targeted killing of a terrorist may seem the most expedient course of action in some cases, it is clear that the termination of a person who may hold valuable information (potentially far out of proportion to his own value within an organization) could prove counterproductive when considering the prosecution of a long-term counterterrorist campaign.

Political Repercussions

The last element considered in this section is the potential for negative political repercussions. While states commonly reserve the right to self-defence, the unique nature of terrorism (namely, the likelihood that wanted terrorists may flee beyond the borders of the state) can sometimes mandate that states consider conducting operations outside their own sovereign territory. Due to the potential for overwhelming political fallout, not to mention the possibility of inciting a wider conflict with a neighbor, it is rare that a state will risk authorizing such operations.

Following Israel's killing of Sheikh Yassin, France, Germany, and the United Kingdom vociferously condemned the attack.[96] Of the major world powers, only the United States refused to condemn the attack, citing Yassin's involvement with terrorism and Israel's 'right to self-defence.'[97] Prominent non-governmental organizations, such as Amnesty International, also condemned the attack, stating that, 'once again Israel has chosen to violate international law instead of using alternative lawful means' and that 'the assassination of Sheikh Yassin is likely to further escalate the spiral of violence.'[98]

To further compound Israel's public 'black eye', the Algerian government on March 23, one day after the attack, sponsored a draft resolution in the United Nations Security Council (UNSC) condemning Israel for its actions. Eleven members of the UNSC voted in favour, three abstained, though the United States ultimately quashed the resolution by exercising its veto powers.[99] [100] This did not preclude UN Secretary General Kofi Annan from publicly condemning the attack: 'Such actions are not only contrary to international law, but they do not do anything to help the search for a peaceful solution.'[101]

Clearly, such overt targeted killings do not go unnoticed on the world stage. States must be willing to risk the most severe forms of international condemnation (for example, UN resolutions, the possible risk of treaty pullouts, economic sanctions) should they choose to pursue targeted killing as a tool in their counterterrorism arsenals.

Case Study: The 1972 Munich Olympics and the Israeli Response
Perhaps the most notable example of a targeted killing campaign that resulted in negative international

repercussions was conducted by Israel following the 1972 Munich Olympics. This case study provides an example of the potentially disastrous consequences when states partake in unilateral actions (particularly prolonged actions) against perceived or known individual terrorist threats. While a detailed examination of the Black September operation and the complex events surrounding it are beyond the scope of this book, the relevance of this particular event merits special attention here, and for that reason, will be discussed in greater detail than in the previously outlined case studies.

In September 1972, a team of eight heavily armed terrorists from the pro-Palestinian group Black September attacked an apartment block housing Israeli athletes in Munich, Germany.[102] In the resulting action, the terrorists killed two athletes outright, and took nine hostages. Protracted negotiations ensued, involving representatives from numerous countries, including Egypt, Germany, and Israel. During this time, the entire event was televised worldwide to an audience of hundreds of millions— thus granting the terrorists the audience they so greatly desired.

These negotiations resulted in an agreement by which the terrorists would be granted safe passage out of Germany. However, upon arrival at the airport, German police opened fire. In the ensuing gun battle, all Israeli hostages, five of the eight terrorists, and one German policeman were killed. Three of the terrorists were taken into custody, though soon released, when Palestinian terrorists hijacked a Lufthansa flight and demanded the safe return of their imprisoned comrades.[103]

In the aftermath of the attack, senior Israeli officials (including Prime Minister Golda Meir) decided to form a covert action team to track down and kill those individuals who participated and planned the operation. The team was given permission to operate worldwide in its efforts to fulfill its mission. The operatives were selected from both the military special forces and intelligence (Mossad) communities and hand picked for their ability to operate covertly and their willingness to undertake missions resulting in the targeted killing of their prey. Among these were personnel from the elite Sayeret Matkal counterterrorism unit, equivalent in the West to Great Britain's SAS and Russia's Spetznaz ('spetsialnoye nazranie,' or 'special purpose troops').

It is indeed rare for a state to sanction official targeted killing teams with a global mission. It is more rare still for this sanction to come from the highest level of a state government.[104]   Such was the sentiment in Israel at the time, the public bursting with outrage over the atrocity, that Meir recognized that the actions of Black September could not go unanswered. "We will smite them wherever they may be," she stated in an address to the Knesset soon after the attack.[105]

In the months that followed, the Israeli team hunted down and killed numerous members of Black September around the world, in Lebanon, Italy, and France. It was in Norway, however, that the Israeli operation unraveled. In the mistaken belief that it had tracked down one of its most wanted terrorists, Ali Hassan Salameh, a small team of Mossad operators gunned down an individual on a public street in Lillehammer, Norway. The dead man turned out not to be Salameh, but rather Ahmed Bouchiki, a Moroccan waiter who was returning from a cinema with his pregnant wife. Simon Reeve, in *One Day in September*, describes the shooting and the events that followed as 'one of the greatest disasters in the history of the Mossad.'[106]

Norwegian authorities soon arrested many of the team who had participated in the incident, some of whom were later sentenced to prison terms. Their confessions led to arrests in France, a public trial in Norway, and worse for the leadership in Tel Aviv, exposure of Israel's blatant disregard for national borders and outrage at conducting an illegal targeted killing on foreign soil.

In the end, the retaliatory missions launched by Israel did eventually result in the deaths of most Black September terrorists involved in the Munich massacre; the killings were conducted in secrecy and with plausible deniability to distance Israel from the actions. However, the Lillehammer disaster not only exposed Israel's secret intelligence network to public scrutiny, but more importantly prompted deterioration in its international prestige, leading to significant political fallout.

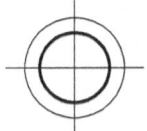

Conclusions

Targeted killing has always been and will remain a double-edged sword. While states may need or choose to eliminate known or perceived threats posed by individuals, the risks, as stated previously, can be immense. There are a number of important conclusions we can draw from the arguments and case studies cited in this book. First, the practice of targeted killing will continue into the foreseeable future, with states prepared to risk political capital and collateral damage in order enforce their perceptions of self-defence. Second, this practice will remain controversial in the legal battlefields of the UN, The Hague, and in other centres of international legal order and debate. It remains for each individual state to decide if the risks of targeted killing are worth the rewards.

On a more practical level, however, it appears that targeted killing, as a tool of counterterrorism, is a weapon of only limited strategic utility. There is little evidence to indicate that the killing of a specific individual, no matter how high ranking, will have a lasting impact on that group's ability and willingness to continue to wage a terrorist campaign. This is particularly true for those groups with widely shared ideologies and characteristics, long operational histories, and a wide member and support bases. Conversely, it must be stated, targeted killing may be more effective when employed against smaller groups or those less well established and more reliant on a single leader or leaders for their ongoing operations.

Targeted killing does, on the other hand, offer states a method of dealing tactical and operational blows against terrorist targets. This is particularly true in the case of interdicting terrorists known to be preparing or undertaking an imminent terrorist attack. Additionally, the elimination of terrorists who contribute specific and hard-to-replace skills may also impact groups in the short to medium term.

At best, the results of state campaigns of targeted killing have been mixed. In some cases, it is certain that the elimination of individuals has disrupted both imminent attacks and planned future attacks. In other cases, this tool appears to have been used in a preventative sense—eliminating individuals involved with terrorism (for example, the SAS ambush at Loughall), but with no evidence to indicate that they represent a clear and present threat (Sheik Yassin).

Clearly, terrorism presents states with security challenges that differ greatly from those posed by conventional warfare. States have been forced to adapt to these challenges. This has involved the modification of existing laws, the creation of new laws, the development and deployment of specialized military and security units, as well as new technologies designed to assist these forces. Equally as controversial as some of these adaptations have been, so to has been the adoption of contentious and politically risky policies that hinge specifically on the already debatable concepts of anticipatory self-defence and preemption.

As we have seen, the majority of states have not chosen to appeal to the UN for justification in defending themselves from terrorism (at least not on a case by case basis, and certainly not in terms of seeking permission) in those cases in which targeted killing was applied. States have, instead, chosen to allow vague guidelines, such as citing Article 51, to justify their offensive counterterrorist campaigns. This vagueness permits states to operate in a grey world in which they are able to cross national boundaries, both in terms of sovereign borders and international agreements. In the final analysis, it is interesting to note that Israel, the most prolific and experienced practitioner of targeted killing, is the only state known to have made an official effort to set out the conditions in which its military may conduct such operations.[107]

However, as already noted, the ongoing terrorist quest for methods of attack that will cause mass casualties may alter the landscape on which we have, to date, viewed targeted killing. So to many, the fear of terrorists flying a jetliner into a nuclear power plant or chemical farm causes justifiable concern. As the potential risk of massive loss of life at the hands of even one terrorist becomes more realistic, it is likely that states will adopt more flexible approaches to self-defence. Targeted killing, still considered an internationally debatable method of preemptive action, may become less of an ill-thought of arm of counterterrorism, and more valued as a potentially efficient and effective method of self-defence.

Inevitably, states will still have to consider the immeasurable and innumerable possible consequences of embarking on even a single targeted killing operation due to the reasons cited above, namely the potential for collateral damage, martyrdom, and political fallout. It is this debate—the risk versus the reward—that states will have to consider as they seek new and potentially controversial methods to defend themselves from the spectre of terrorism or opt to continue their agenda of targeted killing.

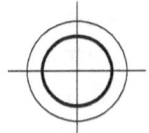

Selected Bibliography

Adkins, Roy, *Trafalgar: The Biography of a Battle* (Great Britain: Little, Brown, 2004)

Asher, Michael, *Get Rommel: The Secret British Mission to Kill Hitler's Greatest General* (London: The Orion Publishing Group Ltd., 2004)

Bennett, Geoffrey, *The Battle of Trafalgar* (Great Britain: Pen & Sword Military Classics, 2004)

Buckley, Mary, and Fawn, Rick, *Global Responses to Terrorism* (London: Routledge, 2003)

Clausewitz, Carl von, *On War* (Great Britain: Wordsworth Editions Limited, 1997)

Conboy, Kenneth, *Shadow War: The CIA's Secret War in Laos* (USA: Paladin Press, 1995)

Connor, Ken, *Ghost Force: The Secret History of the SAS* (London: Cassell, 1998)

Corbin, Jane, *The Base: Al Qaeda and the Changing Face of Global Terror* (Great Britain: Simon and Schuster UK Ltd, 2003)

Daftary, Farhad, *The Assassin Legends: Myths of the Isma'ilis* (London: I.B. Tauris, 1994)

Dinstein, Yoram, *War, Aggression, and Self-Defence* (Cambridge: Cambridge University Press, 2001)

Franck, Thomas, *Recourse to Force: State Action Against Threats and Armed Attacks* (Cambridge: Cambridge University Press, 2004)

Freedman, Lawrence, *Deterrence* (UK: Polity Press, 2004)

Glad, Betty and Dolan, Chris (eds.), *Striking First: The Preventative War Doctrine and the Reshaping of U.S. Foreign Policy* (New York: Palgrave McMillan, 2004)

Gunaratna, Rohan, *Inside Al Qaeda: Global Network of Terror* (London: Hurst and Company, 2002)

Hammel, Eric, *Six Days in June: How Israel Won the 1967 Arab-Israeli War* (New York: ibooks, inc., 1992)

Harclerode, Peter, *Fighting Dirty: The Inside Story of Covert Operations from Ho Chi Minh to Osama bin Ladin* (London: Cassell, 2001)

Howard, Russell D., and Sawyer, Reid L. (eds.), *Terrorism and Counterterrorism: Understanding the New Security Environment* (USA: McGraw-Hill/Dushkin, 2002)

Hyams, Edward, *Killing No Murder: A Study of Assassination as a Political Means* (Great Britain: Panther Modern Society, 1970)

Kegley, Charles W., *The New Global Terrorism: Characteristics, Causes, Controls* (New Jersey: Prentice Hall, 2003)

Laquer, Walter, *The New Terrorism: Fanaticism and the Arms of Mass Destruction* (Oxford: Oxford University Press, 1999)

Laquer, Walter, (ed.) *Voices of Terror* (Canada: Reed Press, 2004)

Levite, Ariel, *Intelligence and Strategic Surprises* (New York: Colombia University Press, 1987)

Long, David E., *The Anatomy of Terrorism* (New York, The Free Press, 1990)

Longford, Elizabeth, *Wellington: The Years of the Sword* (New York: Harper and Row, 1969)

MacDonald, Callum, *The Killing of SS Obergurppenführer Reinhard Heydrich* (London: Macmillan, 1989)

Meir, Golda, *My Life* (New York: Dell Publishing, 1975)

Netanyahu, Benjamin, *Fighting Terrorism* (New York: Farrar, Straus and Giroux, 2001)

Netanhayu, Iddo, *Entebbe: A Defining Moment in the War on Terrorism* (USA: New Leaf Press, 2003)

O'Sullivan, Noel (ed.), *Terrorism, Ideology, and Revolution: The Origins of Political Violence* (Colorado, USA: Westview Press, 1986)

Ostrovsky, Peter and Hoy, Claire, *By Way of Deception* (New York: St. Martin's Press, 1990)

Pillar, Paul R., *Terrorism and U.S. Foreign Policy* (Washington, D.C.: Brookings Institute Press, 2001)

Pugliese, David, *Canada's Secret Commandos* (Canada: Esprit de Corps, 2002)

Reeve, Simon, *One Day in September* (England: Faber and Faber Ltd., 2000)

Rodin, David, *War & Self-Defence* (Oxford: Clarendon Press, 2002)

Rowan, Brian, *Behind the Lines: The Story of the IRA and Loyalist Ceasefires* (Belfast: The Blackstaff Press Limited, 1995)

Ryan, Mike, *Special Operations in Iraq* (Great Britain: Pen and Sword Military, 2004)

Stevenson, William, *90 Minutes at Entebbe* (USA: Bantam Books, 1976)

Turner, Stansfield, *Terrorism & Democracy* (Boston: Houghton Mifflin, 1991)

Wilkinson, Paul, *Terrorism: British Perspectives* (England: Dartmouth Publishing Company Limited, 1993)

Wilkinson, Paul, *Terrorism Versus Democracy: The Liberal State Response* (Great Britain: Frank Cass Publishing, 2005)

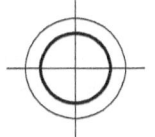

Appendix A

Selected International Incidents of Targeted Killing: 1973-2004

Date	Primary Target(s)	Method	Location	Perpetrator[108]	Result
17 Apr 04	Abd al-Aziz al-Rantisi, successor to Sheikh Yassin	IAF Apache helicopter using guided missiles	Gaza City	Israel[109]	Target killed
22 Mar 04	Sheikh Ahmed Yassin, HAMAS spiritual leader	IAF Apache helicopter using guided missiles	Gaza City	Israel[110]	Target killed, six others killed, more than 20 injured

13 Feb 04	Zelimkhan Yanderbiyev, former Chechen president	Booby-trapped car	Qatar	Russia[111]	Target killed, along with two bodyguards
03 Nov 02	Qaed Senyan al-Harithi, al Qaeda senior operative	U.S. Predator drone, equipped with guided missiles	Yemen	U.S.[112]	Target killed, along with five passengers
19 Mar 02	Chechen warlord Omar Ibn al-Khattab	Letter impregnated with unidentified poison	Chechnya	Russia, via Federal Security Service (FSB)[113]	Target killed
18 Oct 2001	Atef Abayat, senior member of al-Aqsa Martyrs' Brigade	Booby-trapped car	Israel, near Bethlehem	Israel[114]	Target killed, along with two passengers
21 Apr 96	Chechen warlord Dzohkar Dudayev	Guided missile[115]	Chechnya	Russia[116]	Target killed

07 Mar 88	Three members of the Irish Republican Army (IRA)	Small arms	Gibraltar, UK	UK, via Special Air Service (SAS)[117]	All three targets killed
08 May 87	Eight members of the Irish Republican Army (IRA)	Small arms	Loughall, Northern Ireland	UK, via Special Air Service (SAS)[118]	All eight targets killed
10 Apr 73	Yusuf al-Najjar, head of Fatah intelligence arm;	Clandestine commando operations	Beirut, Lebanon	Israel[119]	All targets killed

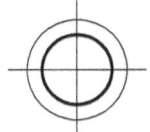

Endnotes

1   See Gal Luft, 'The Logic of Israel's Targeted Killing,' *Middle East Quarterly*, Winter 2003, Volume X, Number 1.

2   Ibid.

3   David Tucker, 'Counterterrorism and the Perils of Preemption Problems and Command and Control,' in Betty Glad and Chris Dolan (eds.), *Striking First: The Preventative War Doctrine and the Reshaping of U.S. Foreign Policy* (New York: Palgrave McMillan, 2004), pgs. 75-89.

4   See, for example, Murray Clark Havens, et al, *The Politics of Assassination* (New Jersey: Prentice Hall, 1970), pgs. 2-6.

5   Edward Hyams, *Killing No Murder: A Study of Assassination as a Political Means* (Great Britain: Panther Modern Society, 1970), pgs. 39-46.

6   Despite the modern acceptance that the term 'assassin' was derived from the Ismaili sect as cited previously, the author would like to note that there is considerable modern debate as to the legitimacy of assigning the heritage of the term 'assassin' to the Ismaili sect. The primary argument against this is well summarized by Farhad Daftary in *The Assassin Legends: Myths of the Isma'ilis* (London: I.B. Tauris, 1994). In this work, Daftary attributes the misnomer to a convoluted progression of misunderstanding and mistranslation. According to Daftary, 'The western tradition of calling the Nizari Isma'ilis by the name of Assassins can be traced to the Crusaders and their Latin chroniclers as well as other occidental observers...

the name, or more appropriately misnomer, Assassin, which was originally derived under obscure circumstances from variants of the word hashish, the Arabic name for a narcotic product, and which later became the common occidental term for designating the Nizari Isma'ilis, soon acquired a new meaning in European languages; it was adopted as a common noun meaning murderer.' While a complete understanding of this new look into the origins of the term assassin is beyond the scope of this book, the author wishes to acknowledge the ongoing debate as to the proper assignation of the term.

7   The author acknowledges here that the caveat of asymmetric warfare, versus conventional warfare, is essential. In large part, historic kingdoms and states were largely threatened only by parties of roughly equal size and makeup. This is to say, more simply, the primary method of warfare has been state versus state rather than today's more ambiguous threats from individuals and small groups. Therefore, the concept of self-defence was one thought of primarily in those terms (see the cited example of Israel prior to the Six Day War). It is for this reason, clearly, that the concept of targeted killing has only recently entered the lexicon and arena of academic and political discussion.

8   As cited by Steven R. David in his paper 'Israel's Policy of Targeted Killing,' in *Ethics and International Affairs: 2003* (Vol. 17, No. 1), 'there is no established norm against targeted killing, but there is against assassination.' (pg. 115). Mr. David provides an excellent assessment of this differentiation in this book as well (see pgs. 112-116).

9   Ward Thomas, The Ethics of Destruction: Norms and Force in International Relations (New York: Cornell University Press, 2001), pgs. 47-85.

10   The specific prohibition on assassination is found in Executive Order 12333, Parts 2.11 and 2.12. The verbatim text demonstrates the clear guidance: '2.11 *Prohibition on assassination.* No person employed by or acting on behalf of the United States Government shall engage in, or conspire to engage in, assassination. 2.12 *Indirect participation.* No agency of the Intelligence Community shall participate in or request any person to undertake activities forbidden by this order.' Notable, for purposes of this discussion,

is the lack of any definition of assassination in EO 12333, which, it could be argued, leaves the legal guidance vague enough to make targeted killing a viable tool of statecraft. See http:// www.cia.gov/cia/information/eo12333.html

11   In 1970, the U.S. Senate Select Committee to Study Government Operations released its report entitled 'Alleged Assassination Plots Involving Foreign Leaders.' This report concluded that the U.S. was involved in the killings of foreign political leaders, and took part in plans for further such killings. Individuals cited as actual or potential targets included Cuban President Fidel Castro, Dominican leader Rafael Trujillo, and South Vietnamese President Ngo Dinh Diem and his brother, Ngo Dinh Nhu. See *Alleged Assassination Plots Involving Foreign Leaders* (Amsterdam: Fredonia Books, 2001). This document can also be found online in numerous locations, including http://www.aarclibrary.org/publib/church/reports/ir/contents.htm.

12   The author was able to discover at least one U.S. military paper that recommended that selective assassination should be further studied as a possible option for the U.S. government. See 'Selective Assassination as an Instrument of National Policy', (Washington: Loompanics Unlimited, 1990). The author of this study was described as a U.S. Air Force captain, though his name and the ultimate purpose of this study remain unknown. It is the author's opinion that this study was the result of an academic program, possibly undertaken at one of the national war colleges.

13   David Rodin, *War & Self-Defence* (Oxford: Clarendon Press, 2002), pg. 189.

14   Rodin, pg. 190.

15   In August 1998, the Clinton Administration authorized cruise missile strikes against a number of targets in Afghanistan and Sudan. These strikes were carried out partly in retaliation for the earlier terrorist suicide bombings of U.S. Embassies in Kenya and Tanzania. The president later stated that there was 'compelling information they were planning additional terrorist attacks against our citizens and others with the inevitable collateral casualties and ... seeking to acquire chemical weapons and other dangerous weapons.' http://www.cnn.com/US/9808/20/us.strikes.01/

16   http://www.un.org/aboutun/charter/chapter7.htm

17 The author acknowledges here that, in the case of self-defence, states are more likely to act without deferring to the UNSC based on their perception that the threat posed against them is of sufficient concern. This is to say that states will act to ensure their survival, rather than defer to any international body for approval on a course of action.

18 Thomas Franck, *Recourse to Force: State Action Against Threats and Armed Attacks* (Cambridge: Cambridge University Press, 2004), pgs. 97-108.

19 Eric Hammel, *Six Days in June: How Israel Won the 1967 Arab-Israeli War* (New York: ibooks, inc., 1992), pgs.165-171.

20 The evidence which led Israel to war included reconnaissance of enemy positions, observations of troop buildups, belligerent talk from enemy leaders (most notably Egyptian president Gamal Nasser), and other obvious indicators. Perhaps most important and provocative among these, however, was the closure of the Straits of Tiran, which effectively blockaded the politically important Israeli port of Eilat – one of the reasons Israel went to war with Egypt in 1956. See Hammel, pgs. 33-37 and 40-42.

21 UN Security Council Resolution 487 (1981). http://daccessdds. un.org/doc/RESOLUTION/GEN/NR0/418/74/IMG/NR041874. pdf?OpenElement

22 A/RES/37/18, November 18, 1982, http://www.un.org/documents/ ga/res/37/a37r018.htm

23 Franck, pg. 96.

24 A review of the historical literature reveals many discussions and instances of senior military officers refusing to consider the targeted killing of their counterparts in battle. For example, according to one interesting anecdote, the following exchange took place between the Duke of Wellington and a nearby English artilleryman. Upon seeing French general Napoleon Bonaparte across the field of battle, the artilleryman exclaimed, "There's Bonaparte, sir. I think I can reach him. May I fire?" The Duke, aghast at the suggestion, replied, "No, no. Generals commanding armies have something else to do than shoot at one another." See Elizabeth Longford, *Wellington: The Years of the Sword* (New York: Harper and Row, 1969), pg. 472.

25 Geoffrey Bennett, *The Battle of Trafalgar* (Great Britain: Pen & Sword Military Classics, 2004), pg.

26 Whether Admiral Lord Nelson was intentionally singled out as a target prior to or during the battle of Trafalgar is a matter of ongoing debate, though it appears that he may have been targeted once identified by the enemy. According to one account, found in the memoirs of a French sharpshooter who claimed to have fired the fatal shot, 'On the poop (deck) of the English vessel was an officer covered with orders and with only one arm. From what I had heard of Nelson, I had no doubt that it was he.' See Geoffrey Bennett, *The Battle of Trafalgar* (Great Britain: Pen & Sword Military Classics, 2004), pg.206. The author could find no credible evidence that the French had given orders for the purposeful killing of Nelson prior to the engagement and his death appears to have been the legitimate outcome of open warfare at sea. It should also be noted that at least one modern study of Trafalgar concluded that Nelson was killed by a stray or ricocheted bullet. See Roy Adkins, *Trafalgar: The Biography of a Battle* (Great Britain: Little, Brown, 2004), pg. 206.

27 For an excellent accounting of the failed British attempt to kill Rommel, see Michael Asher, *Get Rommel: The Secret British Mission to Kill Hitler's Greatest General* (London: The Orion Publishing Group Ltd., 2004).

28 For a detailed accounting of this operation, the author recommends Callum MacDonald, *The Killing of SS Obergurppenfuhrer Reinhard Heydrich* (London: Macmillan, 1990).

29 Mike Ryan, *Special Operations in Iraq* (Great Britain: Pen & Sword Military, 2004), pgs. 42-46.

30 There is some debate as to whether President Roosevelt himself approved the ambush, though at least two authors have cited messages obtained during their research that appear to verify this claim. It is clear, however, that senior U.S. military commanders approved this mission, to include Admiral Chester Nimitz, commander in chief of the U.S. Pacific Fleet. See Carroll V. Glines, *Attack on Yamamoto* (New York: Orion Books, 1990), pgs. 1-12.

31 See Article 37 as found in the 'Protocol Additional to the Geneva Conventions of 12 August 1949, and relating to the Protection of Victims of International Armed Conflicts (Protocol 1 Adopted on

8 June 1977 by the Diplomatic Conference on the Reaffirmation and Development of International Humanitarian Law applicable in Armed Conflicts'. http://www.unhchr.ch/html/menu3/b/93. htm

32 While the perpetrators were not military personnel, but rather that of an Allied intelligence agency, they were under the operational control of the British military and, as such, their conduct was clearly in violation of the Geneva Convention protocols against the use of perfidy.

33 See   http://www.guardian.co.uk/israel/Story/0,2763,1202273,00. html and http://www.chinadaily.com.cn/english/doc/2004-04/24/ content_325957.htm

34 The incident referred to here occurred on April 5, 1986 when terrorists detonated a two-kilogram improvised explosive device (IED). The resulting blast and fire killed two U.S. servicemen and a Turkish woman and was subsequently cited as the tripwire that brought about Operation El Dorado Canyon.   http://news.bbc. co.uk/1/hi/world/europe/1653848.stm

35 David B. Cohen, "Revisiting El Dorado Canyon," *White House Studies*, Spring 2005, p. 21. http://www.findarticles.com/p/articles/ mi_m0KVD/is_2_5/ai_n16107461/pg_21

36 http://edition.cnn.com/2004/WORLD/africa/09/20/libya. sanctions/

37 See, for example, Major Ralph J. Jodice III, USAF, "El Dorado Canyon: Strategic Strike, National Objectives," Command and Staff College, 1990; and Walter Boyne, "El Dorado Canyon," *Air Force: Journal of the Air Force Association*, March 1999, Vol. 82, No. 3.

38 A 'dirty bomb' is a mix of explosives, such as dynamite or semtex, with radioactive powder or pellets. When the dynamite or other explosives are set off, the blast carries radioactive material into the surrounding area. A dirty bomb cannot create an atomic blast, but rather works by disseminating radioloical material throughout a given area.

39 The U.S.-based Centers for Disease Control (CDC) provide an exhaustive list of such agents, including detailed information on many biological agents that maybe used by terrorists.   http:// www.bt.cdc.gov/agent/agentlist.asp

40 http://www.bt.cdc.gov/agent/agentlistchem-category.asp

41 Walter Laquer, *The New Terrorism: Fanaticism and the Arms of Mass Destruction* (Oxford: Oxford University Press, 1999), pg. 4.

42 See, for example, U.S. Congressional Research Service report 'Nuclear Power Plants: Vulnerability to Terrorist Attack,' dated February 4, 2005. http://www.fas.org/irp/crs/RS21131.pdf

43 In 1986, RAND analyst Bruce Hoffman released an unclassified report entitled 'Terrorism in the United States and the Potential Threat to Nuclear Facilities' (Santa Monica: RAND, 1986) on behalf of the U.S. Department of Energy. This report highlighted many of the same concerns that confronted security officials in the months following 9/11.

44 For the purposes of this book, *anti*terrorism reflects more passive measures such as education, surveillance, liaison training and advising; *counter*terrorism refers to offensive measures to prevent and deter terrorism with active interdiction such as targeting and elimination.

45 It should be noted that some deaths involving Palestinian militants, while appearing to be the work of the Israeli government, are sometimes perpetrated by dissident or warring internal factions of the Palestinian liberation movement.

46 For further information on Israeli assassination and targeting killing involving the Mossad and other special units, see Gordon Thomas, *Gideon's Spies: The Secret History of the Mossad* (Thomas Dune Press, 1999) and Alexander Calahan, "Countering Terrorism: The Israeli Response to the 1972 Munich Olympic Massacre and the Development of Independent Covert Action Teams" (Marine Corps Command and General Staff College, April 1995).

47 Thomas B. Hunter, "The Other SAS: The CIA's Special Activities Staff," *Jane's Intelligence Review*, June 1999, pgs. 52-54.

48 This debate is highlighted in *Ethics and International Affairs: 2003*, Vol. 17, No. 1. Papers of interest in this volume include Steven R. David, "Israel's Policy of Targeted Killing," (pgs.111-126) and the response to this book by Yael Stein, "By Any Name Illegal and Immoral," (pgs. 127-139). The author also recommends the critical discussion of the Israeli policy by Michael L. Gross, 'Fighting by Other Means in the Mideast: a Critical Analysis of Israel's Assassination Policy,' *Political Studies: 2003*, Vol. 51, pgs. 350-368.

49 Amos Harel and Gideon Alon, "IDF Lawyers Set 'Conditions' For Assassination Policy," February 4, 2002. http://www.haaretzdaily. com/hasen/pages/ShArt.jhtml?itemNo=125404

50 Richard Sale, 'Israel to Kill in U.S., Allied Nations,' UPI.com, http:// www.upi.com/view.cfm?storyID=20030115-035849-6156r

51 The most notable case involving Israeli targeted killings across international borders occurred after the massacre of Israeli athletes in Munich during the 1972 Olympic Games. In the days following the attack, the Israeli government met secretly to decide on a course of action to respond to these events. The conclusion of this meeting led to a covert campaign to track down and kill each member of the Black September Organization responsible for planning or participating in the attack. The ensuing campaign led the Mossad hit team to various countries around the world in their pursuit, to include the accidental killing of a civilian in Norway (for which the agents were arrested). In this case, it can be argued that Israel was pursuing an act of self-defence, in eliminating individuals known to have taken part in the planning or execution of terrorist activities against the state. However, it is also reasonable to assume that Israel had ulterior motives in its action: intimidation and revenge. The subsequent hunt for and killing of the Munich Olympics terrorists no doubt caused those who had played a part in the massacre to feel their own sense of terror, in that they had become the hunted rather than the hunter. It also demonstrated to the world that Israel was willing to cross borders and patiently seek out anyone who it felt represented a terrorist threat to the state, though this did ultimately, have negative international repercussions.

52 http://www.nationalreview.com/comment/rosenberg 200403221459.asp

53 http://www.info-france-usa.org/news/statmnts/2004/ yassin_032204.asp

54 CNN.com, 'Source: Israel to end targeted killings', February 4, 2005. http://edition.cnn.com/2005/WORLD/meast/02/03/mideast/

55 Benjamin Netanyahu, *Fighting Terrorism: How Democracies Can Defeat the International Terrorist Network* (New York: Farrar, Straus and Giroux, 2001), pgs. 67-68.

56 Benjamin Netanyahu, *Terrorism: How the West Can Win* (New York: Farrar, Strausand Giroux, 1986) pgs 16-17.

57 This should not be construed to mean that the U.S. has never envisioned a preemptive policy against terrorism. Benjamin Netanyahu, in his book *Fighting Terrorism* (New York: Farrar, Straus, and Giroux, 2001) recounted that, while attending a conference on counterterrorism, he had commented to then-Secretary of State George Shultz that, "It is time to think long, hard, and seriously about a more active means of defence – defence through appropriate preventive or preemptive actions against terrorist groups before they strike.' (pg. 69)

58 For an in-depth analysis of U.S. foreign policy under the Bush Administration, see Betty Glad and Chris J. Dolan, *Striking First* (New York: Palgrave Macmillan, 2004).

59 The full text of this speech can be found at the official White House website (http://www.whitehouse.gov). See specifically http://www.whitehouse.gov/news/releases/2002/06/20020601-3.html

60 Numerous reports indicate that the U.S. attempted to kill Taliban leader Mullah Omar using a Predator UAV equipped with guided missiles. The attack succeeded in destroying a number of vehicles, but Mullah Omar was apparently in a nearby building at the time of the attack, safe from the explosion.

61 Publicly available information indicates that the 'Secretary of State may offer rewards of up to $5 million for information that prevents or favorably resolves acts of international terrorism against U.S. persons or property worldwide.' The *Rewards for Justice* website (http://www.rewardsforjustice.net/) indicates that rewards were paid for information leading to the location of Qusay and Uday Hussein, who were subsequently killed by U.S. military forces (ostensibly as a direct result of the provision of this information). While perhaps not wanted for their involvement in terrorism, this evidence indicated that the U.S. is willing to use such information for purposes of locating and killing specific individuals. It is clear from this example and from this assessment that the purposefully vague language 'information that prevents or favorably resolves acts of international terrorism' leaves the legal door open for U.S. use of this information for purposes of targeted killing. This assessment should not be construed to

indicate that the sole purpose of the rewards program is to provide intelligence to facilitate killings. The program has indeed resulted in the successful arrests and convictions of numerous high profile terrorists, such as Khalid Sheikh Mohammed, Ramzi Yousef, and Mir Amal Kansi. It may be interesting to note that the capture and subsequent conviction of Kansi resulted in his execution on November 14, 2002.

62 Walter Pincus, "U.S. Strike Kills Six in al Qaeda," *Washington Post*, pg. A1, November 6, 2002. This article can also be found online at http://www.washingtonpost.com/ac2/wp-dyn?pagename=articl e&node=&contentId=A5126-2002Nov4&notFound=true

63 Department of Defence News Briefing, November 4, 2004. http:// www.defencelink.mil/transcripts/2002/t11042002_t1104sd.html

64 The USS Cole, a U.S. Navy destroyer, was heavily damaged during an al Qaeda suicide boat attack on October 12, 2000, in the Yemeni port of Aden. The attack killed 17 American sailors and injured 39.

65 These verbatim quotes were drawn from an actual Yellow Card obtained by the author during the course of research for this book.

66 Mark Urban, *Big Boys Rules* (London: Faber and Faber Ltd., 1993), pg. 164.

67 For a detailed accounting of the Loughall incident, see Mark Urban, *Big Boys Rules* (London: Faber and Faber Ltd., 1993), pgs. 224-237.

68 IRA terrorists frequently stole weapons from police facilities in order to augment their own supplies of small arms. Forensic examinations of the weapons used by the IRA at Loughall revealed that they had been used previously in the murders of policemen and soldiers.

69 Urban, pg. 228.

70 Urban, pg. 232.

71 European Court of Human Rights, 'Subject – Matter of Judgments Delivered by the Court in 2001,' pg. 23. Cases cited: No. 24746/95, No. 28883/95, No.30054/96, and No. 37715/97. http://www.echr. coe.int/Eng/EDocs/SUBJECT_MATTER_2001_TABLE.pdf

72 Ibid.

73 This argument does not discount the myriad difficulties that authorities likely would have encountered had they tried to arrest

the terrorists. It is highly unlikely that all eight IRA men would have been in the same location. Indeed, available information indicates that at least some of the terrorists were living in the Republic of Ireland in the days leading up to the attack. Thus, effecting their arrests would have posed considerable difficulty. Moreover, the police did not know exactly who would carry out the attack until the time of the attack itself.

74 In fact, it may be argued that a police or military force that fails to interdict such an individual would be delinquent in its duties. Such was the case in the 1983 terrorist bombing of the U.S. Marine Barracks in Lebanon, in which 243 U.S. personnel were killed.

75 David E. Long, *The Anatomy of Terrorism* (New York: The Free Press, 1990), pgs. 29-64.

76 http://www.rand.org/commentary/120303ND.html

77 Author interview, retired 22 SAS operative. 15 July 2005.

78 Netanyahu, pg. 71.

79 http://news.bbc.co.uk/1/hi/uk/315216.stm

80 See Mark Urban, *Big Boys Rules* (London: Faber and Faber Ltd., 1993).

81 Rohan Gunaratna, *Inside Al Qaeda: Global Network of Terror* (United Kingdom: C. Husrts & Co. Ltd., 2002), pgs. 78-79.

82 The author acknowledges here that al Qaeda is no longer a monolithic organization, such as it may have been described prior to 9/11 and the international military offensive that drove it from its bases in Afghanistan. Today, al Qaida is a loose knit consortium of like-minded Islamic extremists who, though in disparate locations and without a central command and control network, continue to observe these guidelines for operational security.

83 There have been numerous articles, books, and documentaries published that describe the Gibraltar incident in detail. See, for example, "Death on the Rock," a documentary produced for ITV in Great Britain. Further information on this excellent program can be found here: http://www.museum.tv/archives/etv/D/htmlD/deathonthe/deathonthe.htm

84 For example, in a paper published in 2003, Steven R. David, Professor of Political Science at The Johns Hopkins University, noted that between the start of the second *intifadah* in 2000 and the fall of 2002, some 20 Palestinian militants had been killed, though

these attacks had claimed the lives of an estimated 50 innocent bystanders. See Steven R. David, "Israel's Policy of Targeted Killing," *Ethics and International Affairs*, Vol. 17, No. 1, 2003, pg. 111.

85 http://www.cnn.com/2004/WORLD/meast/05/29/mideast/index. html
86 http://www.cbsnews.com/stories/2004/03/22/world/ main607747.shtml
87 http://www.cnn.com/2004/WORLD/meast/04/19/un.rantisi/ index.html;http://www.cnn.com/2004/WORLD/meast/04/17/ mideast.violence/index.html
88 http://archives.cnn.com/2002/WORLD/meast/07/23/mideast/
89 http://archives.cnn.com/2001/WORLD/asiapcf/central/11/28/ret. omar.attack/
90 http://news.bbc.co.uk/1/hi/world/middle_east/1017534.stm
91 The author recognizes here that this incident may not have been a targeted killing, in that it is not known if they were seeking to eliminate a specific individual. The example is used primarily to highlight the innumerable variables present in conducting limited military strikes against specific targets and the potential for unexpected consequences (i.e. the exploding rockets).
92 'Israeli Airstrike on Hamas Van Kills Four,' Associated Press, July 15, 2005. http://news.yahoo.com/s/ap/20050715/ap_on_re_mi_ ea/israel_palestinians_10;_ylt=AreByz8qMA3q4HDpGNR7d0cUvi oA;_ylu=X3oDMTBiMW04NW9mBHNlYwMlJVRPUCUl
93 *The Economist*, "Martyrdom and Murder," January 8, 2004. http:// www.economist.com/opinion/displaystory.cfm?story_id=2329785
94 http://www.globalsecurity.org/military/world/para/ksm.htm
95 A salient example of this occurred in Algeria during the insurgency that occurred between 1954 and 1962. While at first struggling against the Algerian insurgency, the establishment of a robust intelligence organization (Centre de Coordination Interarmees) soon resulted in the arrests and interrogations of thousands of individuals, some of whom were actively involved in acts of terrorism against the French presence there. The intelligence gained from some of these interrogations resulted in effective and efficient action against the insurgents and their supporters. See Peter Harlcerode, *Fighting Dirty* (London: Cassell & Co., 2001), pgs. 211-268.

96 The Times Online, "World leaders condemn Yassin assassination," 22
    March 2004, http://www.timesonline.co.uk/article/0,,1-1047221,00.
    html; CNN.com, "Leaders condemn Yassin killing," 23 March
    2004, http://edition.cnn.com/2004/WORLD/meast/03/22/hamas.
    reaction/; EUBusiness.com, "EU ministers condemn Yassin
    'assassination'," 22 March 2004, http://www.eubusiness.com/
    afp/040322122424.soccqfav.

97 White House Press Briefing, 22 March 2004.   http://www.
    whitehouse.gov/news/releases/2004/03/20040322-4.html

98 Amnesty International press release, "Israel/Occupied Territories:
    Amnesty International strongly condemns the assassination of
    Sheikh Yassin," 22 March 2004. http://web.amnesty.org/library/
    Index/ENGMDE150292004?open&of=ENG-PSE

99 United Nations Press Release, SC/8039, March 25, 2004. http://
    www.un.org/News/Press/docs/2004/sc8039.doc.htm

100 Associated Press, March 23, 2004, 'U.S. Vetoes U.N. Resolution
    Condemning Killing of HAMAS Leader Yassin,' http://www.
    foxnews.com/story/0,2933,115242,00.html.

101 http://www.un.org/apps/sg/offthecuff.asp?nid=564

102 For more thorough recounting of the attack and the ensuing Israeli
    program of targeted killing "Operation Wrath of God," please see
    Simon Reeve, *One Day in September* (England: Faber and Faber
    Ltd., 2000) and Alexander Calahan, "Countering Terrorism: The
    Israeli Response to the 1972 Munich Olympic Massacre and the
    Development of Independent Covert Action Teams," (Marine
    Corps Command and General Staff College, April 1995).

103 Reeve, pgs. 183-186.

104 It is worth noting, also, that Meir herself signed the death warrants
    for those involved in planning or perpetrating the attacks. See
    Reeve, pg. 192 and Victor Ostrovsky and Claire Hoy, *By Way of
    Deception* (New York: St. Martin's Press, 1990), pg. 179.

105 Reeve, pg. 180.

106 Reeve, pg. 229.

107 It is further interesting to note that this codification took place
    only after decades of the 'unregulated' practice of targeted
    killing, and just two years before the policy was redacted by the
    Israeli government.

108 Due to the clandestine nature of many targeted killings, the actual perpetrators of the attack often do not claim direct credit. Thus, the author endeavored to determine the author of the attack in the cases cited in Appendix A, through press reporting and the available literature.

109 http://news.bbc.co.uk/1/hi/world/middle_east/3635755.stm

110 http://edition.cnn.com/2004/WORLD/meast/03/21/yassin/

111 http://www.jamestown.org/terrorism/news/article.php?articleid=2368259

112 http://www.theage.com.au/articles/2002/11/05/1036308311314.html?oneclick=true

113 http://news.bbc.co.uk/2/hi/europe/1952053.stm

114 http://www.tkb.org/KeyLeader.jsp?memID=6282

115 The missile that killed Dudayev was reportedly fired after his location was pinpointed during a satellite phone call. Russian signals intelligence (SIGINT) reportedly intercepted the phone call and passed the coordinates to a Russian missile unit kilometers away, which then engaged the target. See Michal Fiszer, Jerzy Gruszczynski, 'Bolt from the blue: Russian land-based precision-strike missiles,' *Journal of Electronic Defence*, March 1, 2003.

116 http://www.amina.com/article/did_nsa.html

117 http://news.bbc.co.uk/onthisday/hi/dates/stories/september/30/newsid_2542000/2542719.stm

118 http://news.bbc.co.uk/2/hi/talking_point/forum/760385.stm

119 http://www.fas.org/irp/eprint/calahan.htm